THE GIFT

THE GIFT

*Forms and Functions of Exchange
in Archaic Societies*

by

MARCEL MAUSS

Translated by
IAN CUNNISON

With an Introduction by
E. E. EVANS-PRITCHARD
*Professor of Social Anthropology
and Fellow of All Souls College, Oxford*

The Norton Library
W · W · NORTON & COMPANY · INC ·
NEW YORK

First published in the Norton Library 1967 by
arrangement with Routledge & Kegan Paul Ltd.

Published simultaneously in Canada by
George J. McLeod Limited, Toronto

Books That Live
The Norton imprint on a book means that in the publisher's
estimation it is a book not for a single season but for the years.
W. W. Norton & Company, Inc.

PRINTED IN THE UNITED STATES OF AMERICA

1 2 3 4 5 6 7 8 9 0

INTRODUCTION

By E. E. Evans-Pritchard
*Fellow of All Souls College and Professor of Social Anthropology,
University of Oxford*

MARCEL MAUSS (1872–1950), Emile Durkheim's nephew and most distinguished pupil, was a man of unusual ability and learning, and also of integrity and strong convictions. After Durkheim's death he was the leading figure in French sociology. His reputation was closely bound up with the fortunes of the *Année Sociologique* which he helped his uncle to found and make famous; some of the most stimulating and original contributions to its earlier numbers were written by him in collaboration with Durkheim and Hubert and Beuchat: *Essai sur la nature et la fonction du sacrifice* (1899), *De quelques formes primitives de classification: contribution à l'étude des représentations collectives* (1903), *Esquisse d'une théorie générale de la magie* (1904), and *Essai sur les variations saisonnières des sociétés eskimos: essai de morphologie sociale* (1906).

The war of 1914–18, during which Mauss was on operational service, almost wiped out the team of brilliant younger scholars whom Durkheim had taught, inspired, and gathered around him—his son André Durkheim, Robert Hertz, Antoine Bianconi, Georges Gelly, Maxime David, Jean Reynier. The Master did not survive them (d. 1917). Had it not been for these disasters Mauss might have given us in ampler measure the fruits of his erudition, untiring industry, and mastery of method. But he not only wrote about social solidarity and collective sentiments. He expressed them in his own life. For him the group of Durkheim and his pupils and colleagues had a kind of collective mind, the material representation of which was its product the *Année*. And if one belongs to others and not to oneself, which is one of the themes, perhaps the basic theme, of the present book, one expresses one's attachment by sub-ordinating one's own ambitions to the common interest. On the few occasions I met Mauss I received the impression that this was how he thought and felt, and his actions confirmed it. He took over the labours of his dead colleagues. Most un-selfishly, for it meant neglecting his own researches, he under-took the heavy task of editing, completing and publishing the manuscripts left by Durkheim, Hubert (who died in 1927), Hertz and others. He undertook also, in 1923–24, the even heavier task of reviving his beloved *Année*, which had ceased publication after 1913. This imposed an added burden on him and further deflected him from the field of his own chief interest. Mauss became a Sanskrit scholar and a historian of religions at the same time as he became a sociologist, and his main interest throughout his life was in Comparative Religion or the Sociology of Religion. But he felt that the new series of the *Année* must, like the old one, cover all the many branches of sociological research, and this could only be done if he took over those branches other than his own which would have been the special concern of those who had died. Consequently, though he published many reviews and review-articles, his only major works after 1906 were the *Essai sur le don, forme archaïque de l'échange* (1925), which Dr. Cunnison now presents in an English translation, *Fragment d'un plan de sociologie générale descrip-tive* (1934), and *Une catégorie de l'esprit humain: la notion de per-sonne, celle de 'moi'* (1938). His projected works on Prayer, on Money and on the State were never completed. But he was active all the time. The second series of the *Année* had to be abandoned, but a third series was started in 1934. Then came the war of 1939–45. Paris was occupied by the Nazis, and Mauss was a Jew. He was not himself injured, but some of his closest colleagues and friends, Maurice Halbwachs and others, were killed. For a second time he saw all around him collapse, and this, combined with other and personal troubles, was too much for him and his mind gave way.

This is not the place to make a critical assessment of Mauss's part in the development of sociological thought in France—it has been admirably done by Henri Lévy-Bruhl and Claude Lévi-Strauss.* All that is required are some very brief indications of the importance of Mauss's work and of the *Essai sur le don* as a particular example of it.

Mauss was in the line of philosophical tradition running from Montesquieu through the philosophers of the Enlightenment—Turgot, Condorcet, St. Simon—to Comte and then Durkheim, a tradition in which conclusions were reached by analysis of concepts rather than of facts, the facts being used as illustrations of formulations reached by other than inductive methods. But while that is true, it is also true that Mauss was far less a philosopher than Durkheim. In all his essays he turns first to the concrete facts and examines them in their entirety and to the last detail. This was the main theme of an excellent lecture on Mauss delivered recently (1952) at Oxford by one of his former pupils, M. Louis Dumont. He pointed out that though Mauss, out of loyalty and affection, studiously avoided any criticism of Durkheim such criticism is nevertheless implicit in his writings, which are so much more empirical than Durkheim's that it might be said that with Mauss sociology in France reached its experimental stage. Mauss sought only to know a limited range of facts and then to understand them, and what Mauss meant by understanding comes out very clearly in this Essay. It is to see social phenomena—as, indeed, Durkheim taught that they should be seen—in their totality. 'Total' is the key word of the Essay. The exchanges of archaic societies which he examines are total social movements or activities. They are at the same time economic, juridical, moral, aesthetic, religious, mythological and socio-morphological phenomena. Their meaning can therefore only be grasped if they are viewed as a complex concrete reality, and if for convenience we make abstractions in studying some institution we

* H. Lévy-Bruhl, 'In Memoriam: Marcel Mauss' in *L'Année Sociologique*, Troisième Série, 1948–49. C. Lévi-Strauss, 'La Sociologie française' in *La sociologie au XXᵉ siècle*, 1947, Vol. 2 (*Twentieth Century Sociology*, 1946, ch. xvii); 'Introduction a l'oeuvre de Marcel Mauss', in *Sociologie et Anthropologie*, a collection of some of Mauss's essays published in 1950.

must in the end replace what we have taken away if we are to understand it. And the means to be used to reach an understanding of institutions? They are those employed by the anthropological fieldworker who studies social life from both outside and inside, from the outside as anthropologist and from the inside by identifying himself with the members of the society he is studying. Mauss demonstrated that, given enough well documented material, he could do this without leaving his flat in Paris. He soaked his mind in ethnographical material, including all available linguistic material; but he was successful only because that mind was also a master of sociological method. Mauss did in his study what an anthropologist does in the field, bringing a trained mind to bear on the social life of primitive peoples which he both observes and experiences. We social anthropologists therefore regard him as one of us.

But to understand 'total' phenomena in their totality it is necessary first to know them. One must be a scholar. It is not sufficient to read the writings of others about the thought and customs of ancient India or ancient Rome. One must be able to go straight to the sources, for scholars not trained in sociological methods will not have seen in the facts what is of sociological significance. The sociologist who sees them in their totality sees them differently. Mauss was able to go to the sources. Besides having an excellent knowledge of several modern European languages, including Russian, he was a fine Greek, Latin, Sanskrit, Celtic and Hebrew scholar, as well as a brilliant sociologist. Perhaps to their surprise, he was able to teach Sanskritists much that they did not know was in their texts and Roman lawyers much that they did not know was in theirs. What he says about the meaning of certain forms of exchange in ancient India and in ancient Rome in the *Essai sur le don* is an illustration. This was perhaps not so remarkable a feat as that he was able to show from Malinowski's own account of the Trobriand Islanders where he had misunderstood, or had inadequately understood, their institutions. He could do this because of his vast knowledge, which Malinowski lacked, of Oceanic languages and of the native societies of

Melanesia, Polynesia, America and elsewhere, which enabled him to deduce by a comparative study of primitive institutions what the fieldworker had not himself observed.

The *Essai sur le don*, apart from its value as an exercise in method, is a precious document in itself. It is of great importance for an understanding of Mauss and for an assessment of his significance as a scholar, since most of his other well-known Essays were written in collaboration, but it is also of great intrinsic value. It is the first systematic and comparative study of the widespread custom of gift exchange and the first understanding of its function in the articulation of the social order. Mauss shows in this Essay what is the real nature, and what is the fundamental significance, of such institutions as the *potlatch* and the *kula* which at first sight bewilder us or even seem to be pointless and unintelligible. And when he shows us how to understand them he reveals not only the meaning of certain customs of North American Indians and of Melanesians but at the same time the meaning of customs in early phases of historical civilizations; and, what is more, the significance of practices in our own society at the present time. In Mauss's Essays there is always implicit a comparison, or contrast, between the archaic institutions he is writing about and our own. He is asking himself not only how we can understand these archaic institutions but also how an understanding of them helps us the better to understand our own, and perhaps to improve them. Nowhere does this come out more clearly than in the *Essai sur le don*, where Mauss is telling us, quite pointedly, in case we should not reach the conclusion for ourselves, how much we have lost, whatever we may have otherwise gained, by the substitution of a rational economic system for a system in which exchange of goods was not a mechanical but a moral transaction, bringing about and maintaining human, personal, relationships between individuals and groups. We take our own social conventions for granted and we seldom think how recent many of them are and how ephemeral they will perhaps prove to be. Men at other times had, and in many parts of the world still have, different ideas, values and customs, from a study of which we may learn much that, Mauss believed, may be of value to ourselves.

It is some years since I suggested to Dr. Cunnison that he might translate this Essay of Marcel Mauss. A good knowledge of French is, of course, essential, but it is not in itself sufficient for the translation of a sociological work from French into English. The translator must be also a sociologist, or in the case of Mauss better still a social anthropologist; for to translate the words is one thing, to translate them in the sense of the author is another. Dr. Cunnison has both requirements. He is a French scholar and also an anthropologist. The translation and its publication have been delayed by the need for revision, and it is greatly to Dr. Cunnison's credit that he has found time to complete his task in the midst of his own considerable anthropological researches carried out during the last few years, first among the Luapula peoples of Northern Rhodesia and then, without respite, among the Baggara Arabs of the Anglo-Egyptian Sudan.

TRANSLATOR'S NOTE

THE editing of this translation differs from that of the original French edition in a number of ways which it is hoped will make for easier reading. In the French edition the compendious notes were printed on the text pages. Here they are placed after the text and numbered separately by chapters. Some short notes have been combined for the sake of clarity but each note still refers to a single subject. Bibliographical references have been standardized throughout the notes. The whole text is printed in type of the same size whereas some sections of the original are in smaller type than the main body of the text. Finally, the orthographic refinements of Indian and North-West American words have not been reproduced.

Mauss used the words *don* and *présent* indifferently, and here similarly 'gift' and 'present' are used for the most part interchangeably, although 'gift' may have the more formal meaning. There is no convenient English word to translate the French *prestation* so this word itself is used to mean any thing or series of things given freely or obligatorily as a gift or in exchange; and includes services, entertainments, etc., as well as material things.

I. C.

CONTENTS

I have never found a man so generous and hospitable that he would not receive a present, nor one so liberal with his money that he would dislike a reward if he could get one.

Friends should rejoice each others' hearts with gifts of weapons and raiment, that is clear from one's own experience. That friendship lasts longest—if there is a chance of its being a success—in which friends both give and receive gifts.

A man ought to be a friend to his friend and repay gift with gift. People should meet smiles with smiles and lies with treachery.

Know—if you have a friend in whom you have sure confidence and wish to make use of him, you ought to exchange ideas and gifts with him and go to see him often.

If you have another in whom you have no confidence and yet will make use of him, you ought to address him with fair words but crafty heart and repay treachery with lies.

Further, with regard to him in whom you have no confidence and of whose motives you are suspicious, you ought to smile upon him and dissemble your feelings. Gifts ought to be repaid in like coin.

Generous and bold men have the best time in life and never foster troubles. But the coward is apprehensive of everything and a miser is always groaning over his gifts.

Better there should be no prayer than excessive offering; a gift always looks for recompense. Better there should be no sacrifice than an excessive slaughter.

> *Havamal*, vv. 39, 41–2, 44–6, 48 and 145, from the translation by D. E. Martin Clarke in *The Havamal, with Selections from other Poems in the Edda*, Cambridge, 1923.

GIFTS AND RETURN GIFTS

THE foregoing lines from the *Edda* outline our subject-matter.[1] In Scandinavian and many other civilizations contracts are fulfilled and exchanges of goods are made by means of gifts. In theory such gifts are voluntary but in fact they are given and repaid under obligation.

This work is part of a wider study. For some years our attention has been drawn to the realm of contract and the system of economic prestations between the component sections or sub-groups of 'primitive' and what we might call 'archaic' societies. On this subject there is a great mass of complex data. For, in these 'early' societies, social phenomena are not discrete; each phenomenon contains all the threads of which the social fabric is composed. In these *total* social phenomena, as we propose to call them, all kinds of institutions find simultaneous expression: religious, legal, moral, and economic. In addition, the phenomena have their aesthetic aspect and they reveal morphological types.

We intend in this book to isolate one important set of phenomena: namely, prestations which are in theory voluntary, disinterested and spontaneous, but are in fact obligatory and interested. The form usually taken is that of the gift generously offered; but the accompanying behaviour is formal pretence and social deception, while the transaction itself is based on obligation and economic self-interest. We shall note the various principles behind this necessary form of exchange (which is nothing less than the division of labour itself), but we shall confine our detailed study to the enquiry: *In primitive or archaic types of society what is the principle whereby the gift received has to be repaid? What force is there in the thing given which compels the recipient to make a return?* We hope, by presenting enough data, to be able to answer this question precisely, and also to indicate the direction in which answers to cognate questions might be sought. We shall also pose new problems. Of these, some concern the morality of the contract: for instance, the manner in which today the law of things remains bound up with the law of persons; and some refer to the forms and ideas which have always been present in exchange and which even now are to be seen in the idea of individual interest.

Thus we have a double aim. We seek a set of more or less archaeological conclusions on the nature of human transactions in the societies which surround us and those which immediately preceded ours, and whose exchange institutions differ from our own. We describe their forms of contract and exchange. It has been suggested that these societies lack the economic market, but this is not true; for the market is a human phenomenon which we believe to be familiar to every known society. Markets are found before the development of merchants, and before their most important innovation, currency as we know it. They functioned before they took the modern forms (Semitic, Hellenic, Hellenistic, and Roman) of contract and sale and capital. We shall take note of the moral and economic features of these institutions.

We contend that the same morality and economy are at work, albeit less noticeably, in our own societies, and we believe that in them we have discovered one of the bases of social life; and thus we may draw conclusions of a moral nature about some of the problems confronting us in our present economic crisis. These pages of social history, theoretical sociology, political economy and morality do no more than lead us to old problems which are constantly turning up under new guises.[2]

THE METHOD FOLLOWED

Our method is one of careful comparison. We confine the study to certain chosen areas, Polynesia, Melanesia, and North-West America, and to certain well-known codes. Again, since we are concerned with words and their meanings, we choose only areas where we have access to the minds of the societies through documentation and philological research. This further limits our field of comparison. Each particular study has a bearing on the systems we set out to describe and is presented in its logical place. In this way we avoid that method of haphazard comparison in which institutions lose their local colour and documents their value.

PRESTATION, GIFT AND POTLATCH

This work is part of the wider research carried out by M. Davy and myself upon archaic forms of contract, so we may start by summarizing what we have found so far.[3] It appears that there has never existed, either in the past or in modern primitive societies, anything like a 'natural' economy.[4] By a strange chance the type of that economy was taken to be the one described by Captain Cook when he wrote on exchange and barter among the Polynesians.[5] In our study here of these same Polynesians we shall see how far removed they are from a state of nature in these matters.

In the systems of the past we do not find simple exchange of goods, wealth and produce through markets established among individuals. For it is groups, and not individuals, which carry on exchange, make contracts, and are bound by obligations;[6] the persons represented in the contracts are moral persons—clans, tribes, and families; the groups, or the chiefs as intermediaries for the groups, confront and oppose each other.[7] Further, what they exchange is not exclusively goods and wealth, real and personal property, and things of economic value. They exchange rather courtesies, entertainments, ritual, military assistance, women, children, dances, and feasts; and fairs in which the market is but one element and the circulation of wealth but one part of a wide and enduring contract. Finally, although the prestations and counter-prestations take place under a voluntary guise they are in essence strictly obligatory, and their sanction is private or open warfare. We propose to call this the system of *total prestations*. Such institutions seem to us to be best represented in the alliance of pairs of phratries in Australian and North American tribes, where ritual, marriages, succession to wealth, community of right and interest, military and religious rank and even games [8] all form part of one system and presuppose the collaboration of the two moieties of the tribe. The Tlingit and Haida of North-West America give a good expression of the nature of these practices when they say that they 'show respect to each other'.[9]

But with the Tlingit and Haida, and in the whole of that region, total prestations appear in a form which, although quite typical, is yet evolved and relatively rare. We propose, following American authors, to call it the *potlatch*. This Chinook word has passed into the current language of Whites and Indians from Vancouver to Alaska. Potlatch meant originally 'to nourish' or 'to consume'.[10] The Tlingit and Haida inhabit the islands, the coast, and the land between the coast and the Rockies; they are very rich, and pass their winters in continuous festival, in banquets, fairs and markets which at the same time are solemn tribal gatherings. The tribes place themselves hierarchically in their fraternities and secret societies. On these occasions are practised marriages, initiations, shamanistic seances, and the cults of the great gods, totems, and group or individual ancestors. These are all accompanied by ritual and by prestations by whose means political rank within sub-groups, tribes, tribal confederations and nations is settled.[11] But the remarkable thing about these tribes is the spirit of rivalry and antagonism which dominates all their activities. A man is not afraid to challenge an opposing chief or nobleman. Nor does one stop at the purely sumptuous destruction of accumulated wealth in order to eclipse a rival chief (who may be a close relative).[12] We are here confronted with total prestation in the sense that the whole clan, through the intermediacy of its chiefs, makes contracts involving all its members and everything it possesses.[13] But the agonistic character of the prestation is pronounced. Essentially usurious and extravagant, it is above all a struggle among nobles to determine their position in the hierarchy to the ultimate benefit, if they are successful, of their own clans. This agonistic type of total prestation we propose to call the 'potlatch'.

So far in our study Davy and I had found few examples of this institution outside North-West America,[14] Melanesia, and Papua.[15] Everywhere else—in Africa, Polynesia, and Malaya, in South America and the rest of North America—the basis of exchange seemed to us to be a simpler type of total prestation. However, further research brings to light a number of forms intermediate between exchanges marked by exaggerated rivalry like those of the American north-west and Melanesia, and others more moderate where the contracting parties rival each other with gifts: for instance, the French compete with each other in their ceremonial gifts, parties, weddings, and invitations, and feel bound, as the Germans say, to *revanchieren* themselves.[16] We find some of these intermediate forms in the Indo-European world, notably in Thrace.[17]

Many ideas and principles are to be noted in systems of this type. The most important of these spiritual mechanisms is clearly the one which obliges us to make a return gift for a gift received. The moral and religious reasons for this constraint are nowhere more obvious than in Polynesia; and in approaching the Polynesian data in the following chapter we shall see clearly the power which enforces the repayment of a gift and the fulfilment of contracts of this kind.

CHAPTER I

GIFTS AND THE OBLIGATION TO RETURN GIFTS

1. TOTAL PRESTATION
MASCULINE AND FEMININE PROPERTY
(SAMOA)

I N our earlier researches on the distribution of the system
of contractual gifts, we had found no real potlatch in
Polynesia. The Polynesian societies whose institutions came
nearest to it appeared to have nothing beyond a system of total
prestations, that is to say of permanent contracts between clans
in which their men, women and children, their ritual, etc.,
were put on a communal basis. The facts that we had studied,
including the remarkable Samoan custom of the exchange of
decorated mats between chiefs on their marriages, did not
indicate more complex institutions.[1] The elements of rivalry,
destruction and fighting seemed to be absent, although we
found they were present in Melanesia. We now reconsider the
matter in the light of new material.

The system of contractual gifts in Samoa is not confined to
marriage; it is present also in respect of childbirth,[2] circum-
cision,[3] sickness,[4] girls' puberty,[5] funeral ceremonies [6] and
trade.[7] Moreover, two elements of the potlatch have in fact
been attested to: the honour, prestige or *mana* which wealth
confers; [8] and the absolute obligation to make return gifts
under the penalty of losing the *mana*, authority and wealth.[9]

Turner tells us that on birth ceremonies, after receiving the
oloa and the *tonga*, the 'masculine' and 'feminine' property,
'the husband and wife were left no richer than they were.
Still, they had the satisfaction of seeing what they considered
to be a great honour, namely, the heaps of property collected

6

on the occasion of the birth of their child.' [10] These gifts are probably of an obligatory and permanent nature, and returns are made only through the system of rights which compels them. In this society, where cross-cousin marriage is the rule, a man gives his child to his sister and brother-in-law to bring up; and the brother-in-law, who is the child's maternal uncle, calls the child a *tonga*, a piece of feminine property.[11] It is then a 'channel through which native property [12] or *tonga*, continues to flow to that family from the parents of the child. On the other hand, the child is to its parents a source of foreign property or *oloa*, coming from the parties who adopt it, as long as the child lives.' 'This sacrifice of natural ties creates a systematic facility in native and foreign property.' In short, the child (feminine property) is the means whereby the maternal family's property is exchanged for that of the paternal family. Since the child in fact lives with his maternal uncle he clearly has a right to live there and thus has a general right over his uncle's property. This system of fosterage is much akin to the generally recognized right of the sister's son over his uncle's property in Melanesia.[13] We need only the elements of rivalry, fighting and destruction for the complete potlatch.

Now let us consider the terms *oloa* and more particularly *tonga*. The latter means indestructible property, especially the marriage mats [14] inherited by the daughters of a marriage, and the trinkets and talismans which, on condition of repayment, come through the wife into the newly founded family; these constitute real property.[15] The *oloa* designates all the things which are particularly the husband's personal property.[16] This term is also applied today to things obtained from Europeans, clearly a recent extension.[17] We may disregard as inexact and insufficient the translation suggested by Turner of *oloa* as foreign and *tonga* as native; yet it is not without significance, since it suggests that certain property called *tonga* is more closely bound up with the land, the clan and the family than certain other property called *oloa*.[18]

But if we extend our field of observation we immediately find a wider meaning of the notion *tonga*. In the Maori,

Tahitian, Tongan and Mangarevan languages it denotes
everything which may be rightly considered property, which
makes a man rich, powerful or influential, and which can be
exchanged or used as compensation: that is to say, such objects
of value as emblems, charms, mats and sacred idols, and perhaps even traditions, magic and ritual.[19] Here we meet that
notion of magical property which we believe to be widely
spread in the Malayo-Polynesian world and right over the
Pacific.[20]

2. THE SPIRIT OF THE THING GIVEN
(MAORI)

This last remark leads to a contention of some importance.
The *taonga* are, at any rate with the Maori, closely attached to
the individual, the clan and the land; they are the vehicle of
their *mana*—magical, religious and spiritual power. In a
proverb collected by Sir G. Grey [21] and C. O. Davis,[22] *taonga*
are asked to destroy the person who receives them; and they
have the power to do this if the law, or rather the obligation,
about making a return gift is not observed.

Our late friend Hertz saw the significance of this; disinterestedly he had written 'for Davy and Mauss' on the card
containing the following note by Colenso: 'They had a kind of
system of exchange, or rather of giving presents which had
later to be exchanged or repaid.' [23] For example, they exchange
dried fish for pickled birds and mats.[24] The exchange is carried
out between tribes or acquainted families without any kind of
stipulation.

But Hertz had also found—I discovered it amongst his
papers—a text whose significance we had both missed, for
I had been unaware of it myself. Speaking of the *hau*, the spirit
of things and particularly of the forest and forest game, Tamati
Ranaipiri, one of Mr. Elsdon Best's most useful informants,
gives quite by chance the key to the whole problem.[25] 'I shall
tell you about *hau*. *Hau* is not the wind. Not at all. Suppose you
have some particular object, *taonga*, and you give it to me; you

give it to me without a price.[26] We do not bargain over it. Now I give this thing to a third person who after a time decides to give me something in repayment for it (*utu*),[27] and he makes me a present of something (*taonga*). Now this *taonga* I received from him is the spirit (*hau*) of the *taonga* I received from you and which I passed on to him. The *taonga* which I receive on account of the *taonga* that came from you, I must return to you. It would not be right on my part to keep these *taonga* whether they were desirable or not. I must give them to you since they are the *hau* [28] of the *taonga* which you gave me. If I were to keep this second *taonga* for myself I might become ill or even die. Such is *hau*, the *hau* of personal property, the *hau* of the *taonga*, the *hau* of the forest. Enough on that subject.'

This capital text deserves comment. It is characteristic of the indefinite legal and religious atmosphere of the Maori and their doctrine of the 'house of secrets'; it is surprisingly clear in places and offers only one obscurity: the intervention of a third person. But to be able to understand this Maori lawyer we need only say: 'The *taonga* and all strictly personal possessions have a *hau*, a spiritual power. You give me *taonga*, I give it to another, the latter gives me *taonga* back, since he is forced to do so by the *hau* of my gift; and I am obliged to give this one to you since I must return to you what is in fact the product of the *hau* of your *taonga*.'

Interpreted thus not only does the meaning become clear, but it is found to emerge as one of the *leitmotifs* of Maori custom. The obligation attached to a gift itself is not inert. Even when abandoned by the giver, it still forms a part of him. Through it he has a hold over the recipient, just as he had, while its owner, a hold over anyone who stole it.[29] For the *taonga* is animated with the *hau* of its forest, its soil, its homeland, and the *hau* pursues him who holds it.[30]

It pursues not only the first recipient of it or the second or the third, but every individual to whom the *taonga* is transmitted.[31] The *hau* wants to return to the place of its birth, to its sanctuary of forest and clan and to its owner. The *taonga* or its *hau*—itself a kind of individual [32]—constrains a series of users to return some kind of *taonga* of their own, some property or merchandise or labour, by means of feasts, entertainments or gifts of equivalent or superior value. Such a return will give its donor authority and power over the original donor, who now becomes the latest recipient. That seems to be the motivating force behind the obligatory circulation of wealth, tribute and gifts in Samoa and New Zealand.

This or something parallel helps to explain two sets of important social phenomena in Polynesia and elsewhere. We can see the nature of the bond created by the transfer of a possession. We shall return shortly to this point and show how our facts contribute to a general theory of obligation. But for the moment it is clear that in Maori custom this bond created by things is in fact a bond between persons, since the thing itself is a person or pertains to a person. Hence it follows that to give something is to give a part of oneself. Secondly, we are led to a better understanding of gift exchange and total prestation, including the potlatch. It follows clearly from what we have seen that in this system of ideas one gives away what is in reality a part of one's nature and substance, while to receive something is to receive a part of someone's spiritual essence. To keep this thing is dangerous, not only because it is illicit to do so, but also because it comes morally, physically and spiritually from a person. Whatever it is, food, [33] possessions, women, children or ritual, it retains a magical and religious hold over the recipient. The thing given is not inert. It is alive and often personified, and strives to bring to its original clan and homeland some equivalent to take its place.

3. THE OBLIGATION TO GIVE AND THE OBLIGATION TO RECEIVE

To appreciate fully the institutions of total prestation and the potlatch we must seek to explain two complementary factors. Total prestation not only carries with it the obligation to repay gifts received, but it implies two others equally important: the obligation to give presents and the obligation to receive them. A complete theory of the three obligations would include a satisfactory fundamental explanation of this form of contract among Polynesian clans. For the moment we simply indicate the manner in which the subject might be treated.

It is easy to find a large number of facts on the obligation to receive. A clan, household, association or guest are constrained to demand hospitality,[34] to receive presents, to barter[35] or to make blood and marriage alliances. The Dayaks have even developed a whole set of customs based on the obligation to partake of any meal at which one is present or which one has seen in preparation.[36]

The obligation to give is no less important. If we understood this, we should also know how men came to exchange things with each other. We merely point out a few facts. To refuse to give, or to fail to invite, is—like refusing to accept— the equivalent of a declaration of war; it is a refusal of friendship and intercourse.[37] Again, one gives because one is forced to do so, because the recipient has a sort of proprietary right over everything which belongs to the donor.[38] This right is expressed and conceived as a sort of spiritual bond. Thus in Australia the man who owes all the game he kills to his father- and mother-in-law may eat nothing in their presence for fear that their very breath should poison his food.[39] We have seen above that the *taonga* sister's son has customs of this kind in Samoa, which are comparable with those of the sister's son (*vasu*) in Fiji.[40]

In all these instances there is a series of rights and duties about consuming and repaying existing side by side with rights and duties about giving and receiving. The pattern of symmetrical and reciprocal rights is not difficult to understand if we realize that it is first and foremost a pattern of spiritual bonds between things which are to some extent parts of persons, and persons and groups that behave in some measure as if they were things.

All these institutions reveal the same kind of social and psychological pattern. Food, women, children, possessions, charms, land, labour, services, religious offices, rank—everything is stuff to be given away and repaid. In perpetual interchange of what we may call spiritual matter, comprising men and things, these elements pass and repass between clans and individuals, ranks, sexes and generations.

4. GIFTS TO MEN AND GIFTS TO GODS

Another theme plays its part in the economy and morality of the gift: that of the gift made to men in the sight of gods or nature. We have not undertaken the wider study necessary to reveal its real import; for the facts at our disposal do not all come from the areas to which we have limited ourselves; and a strongly marked mythological element which we do not yet fully understand prevents us from advancing a theory. We simply give some indications of the theme.

In the societies of North-East Siberia [41] and amongst the Eskimo of West Alaska [42] and the Asiatic coast of the Behring Straits, the potlatch concerns not only men who rival each other in generosity, and the objects they transmit or destroy, and the spirits of the dead which take part in the transactions and whose names the men bear; it concerns nature as well. Exchanges between namesakes—people named after the same spirits—incite the spirits of the dead, of gods, animals and natural objects to be generous towards them.[43] Men say that gift-exchange brings abundance of wealth. Nelson and Porter have given us good descriptions of these ceremonies and the effect they have on the dead, on the game, the fish and shell-fish of the Eskimo. They are expressively called, in the language of British trappers, the 'Asking Festival' or the 'Inviting-in Festival'.[44] Ordinarily they are not confined within the limits of winter settlements. The effect upon nature has been well shown in a recent work on the Eskimo.[45]

The Yuit have a mechanism, a wheel decorated with all manner of provisions, carried on a greasy pole surmounted with the head of a walrus. The top of the pole protrudes above the tent of which it forms the centre. Inside the tent it is manoeuvred by means of another wheel and is made to turn clockwise like the sun. It would be hard to find a better expression of this mode of thought.[46]

The theme is also to be found with the Koryak and Chukchee of the extreme north-west of Siberia.[47] Both have the potlatch. But it is the maritime Chukchee who, like their Yuit neighbours, practise most the obligatory-voluntary gift-exchanges in the course of protracted thanksgiving ceremonies which follow one after the other in every house throughout the winter. The remains of the festival sacrifice are thrown into the sea or cast to the winds; they return to their original home, taking with them all the game killed that year, ready to return again in the next. Jochelsen mentions festivals of the same kind among the Koryak, although he was present only at the whale festival. The system of sacrifice seems there to be very highly developed.[48]

Bogoras rightly compares these with the Russian *koliada* customs in which masked children go from house to house begging eggs and flour and none dare refuse them. This is a European custom.[49]

The connection of exchange contracts among men with those between men and gods explains a whole aspect of the theory of sacrifice. It is best seen in those societies where contractual and economic ritual is practised between men. Where the men are masked incarnations, often shamanistic, being possessed by the spirit whose name they bear, they act as representatives of the spirits.[50] In that case the exchanges and contracts concern not only men and things but also the sacred beings that are associated with them.[51] This is very evident in Eskimo, Tlingit, and one of the two kinds of Haida potlatch.

There has been a natural evolution. Among the first groups of beings with whom men must have made contracts were the spirits of the dead and the gods. They in fact are the real owners of the world's wealth.[52] With them it was particularly necessary to exchange and particularly dangerous not to; but, on the other hand, with them exchange was easiest and safest.

Sacrificial destruction implies giving something that is to be repaid. All forms of North-West American and North-East Asian potlatch contain this element of destruction.[53] It is not simply to show power and wealth and unselfishness that a man puts his slaves to death, burns his precious oil, throws coppers into the sea, and sets his house on fire. In doing this he is also sacrificing to the gods and spirits, who appear incarnate in the men who are at once their namesakes and ritual allies.

But another theme appears which does not require this human support, and which may be as old as the potlatch itself: the belief that one has to buy from the gods and that the gods know how to repay the price. This is expressed typically by the Toradja of the Celebes. Kruyt tells us that the 'owner' can 'buy' from the spirits the right to do certain things with his or rather 'their' property. Before he cuts his wood or digs his garden or stakes out his house he must make a payment to the gods. Thus although the notion of purchase seems to be little developed in the personal economic life of the Toradja, nevertheless, the idea of purchase from gods and spirits is universally understood.[54]

With regard to certain forms of exchange which we describe later Malinowski remarks on facts of the same order from the Trobriands. A malignant spirit is evoked—a *tauvau* whose body has been found in a snake or a land crab—by means of giving it *vaygu'a* (a precious object used in *kula* exchanges, at once ornament, charm and valuable). This gift has a direct effect on the spirit of the *tauvau*.[55] Again at the *mila-mila* festival,[56] a potlatch in honour of the dead, the two kinds of *vaygu'a*—the *kula* ones and those which Malinowski now describes for the first time as 'permanent' *vaygu'a* [57]—are exposed and offered up to the spirits, who take the shades of them away to the country of the dead; [58] there the spirits rival each other in wealth as men do on their return from a solemn *kula*.[59]

Van Ossenbruggen, who is both a theorist and a distinguished observer, and who lives on the spot, has noted another point about these institutions.[60] Gifts to men and to gods have the further aim of buying peace. In this way evil influences are kept at bay, even when not personified; for a human curse will allow these jealous spirits to enter and kill you and permit evil influences to act, and if you commit a fault towards another man you become powerless against them. Van Ossenbruggen interprets in this way not only the throwing of money over the wedding procession in China, but even bridewealth itself. This is an interesting suggestion which raises a series of points.[61]

We see how it might be possible to embark upon a theory and history of contractual sacrifice. Now this sacrifice pre-supposes institutions of the type we are describing, and con-versely it realizes them to the full, for the gods who give and repay are there to give something great in exchange for something small. Perhaps then it is not the result of pure chance that the two solemn formulas of contract, the Latin *do ut des* and the Sanskrit *dadami se, dehi me* have come down to us through religious texts.[62]

A further note: on Alms

Later in legal and religious evolution man appears once more as representative of the gods and the dead, if indeed he had ever ceased to be so. For instance among the Hausa there is often a fever epidemic when the guinea-corn is ripe, and the only way to prevent it is to give presents of wheat to the poor.[63] Again, among the Hausa of Tripolitania, at the time of the great prayer (*Baban Salla*), the children go round the huts saying: 'Shall I enter?' The reply is: 'Oh prick-eared hare, for a bone one gets service' (the poor man is happy to work for the rich). These gifts to children and poor people are pleasing to the dead.[64] These customs may be Islamic in origin,[65] or Islamic, Negro, European and Berber at the same time.

Here at any rate is the beginning of a theory of alms. Alms are the result on the one hand of a moral idea about gifts and wealth [66] and on the other of an idea about sacrifice. Generos-ity is necessary because otherwise Nemesis will take vengeance upon the excessive wealth and happiness of the rich by giving to the poor and the gods. It is the old gift morality raised to the position of a principle of justice; the gods and spirits consent that the portion reserved for them and destroyed in useless sacrifice should go to the poor and the children. Originally the Arabic *sadaka* meant, like the Hebrew *zedaqa*, exclusively justice, and it later came to mean alms. We can say that the Mishnic era, the time of the victory of the Paupers at Jerusalem, begot the doctrine of charity and alms which later went round the world with Christianity and Islam. It was at this time that the word *zedaqa* changed its meaning, since it does not mean alms in *The Bible*.[67]

The value of the documents and commentaries we have quoted in this chapter is not merely local. Comparison takes us farther afield. For we can say that the basic elements of the potlatch are found in Polynesia even if the complete institution is not found there; [68] in any event gift-exchange is the rule. But to emphasize this theme would simply be a show of erudition if it did not extend beyond Polynesia. Let us now shift the subject and demonstrate that at least the *obligation to give* has a much wider distribution. Then we shall show the distribution of the other types of obligation and demonstrate that our interpretation is valid for several other groups of societies.

CHAPTER II

DISTRIBUTION OF THE SYSTEM: GENEROSITY, HONOUR AND MONEY

THE facts here presented are drawn from various ethnographic areas, whose connecting links it is not our business to follow. From the ethnological point of view the existence of common potlatch traits in the Pacific, in North America and even in North Asia may be readily explained. But the existence of a form of potlatch among pygmies is strange, and no less puzzling are the traces of an Indo-European potlatch. We abstain from all considerations of the method by which the institution has spread. It would be naïve and dangerous to talk of borrowing or independent invention. Moreover, the maps which have been drawn for the sake of such arguments represent no more than our present knowledge or ignorance. Let us then for the moment content ourselves with demonstrating the nature and wide distribution of a single theme. It is for others to reconstruct its history if they can.

1. RULES OF GENEROSITY (ANDAMAN ISLANDS)

Customs of the kind we are discussing are found with the pygmies who, according to Pater Schmidt,[1] are the most primitive of men. In 1906 Radcliffe-Brown observed facts of this order in North Andaman, and described them admirably with reference to inter-group hospitality, visits, festivals and fairs, which present the opportunity for voluntary-obligatory exchanges—in this case of ochre and maritime produce against the produce of the chase. Despite the importance of these exchanges, 'as each local group and indeed each family was able to provide itself with everything that it needed in the way of weapons and utensils . . . the exchange of presents did not serve the same purpose as trade or barter in more developed communities. The purpose that it did serve was a moral one. The object of the exchange was to produce a friendly feeling between the two persons concerned, and unless it did this it failed of its purpose. . . .[2] No one was free to refuse a present offered to him. Each man and woman tried to outdo the others in generosity. There was a sort of amiable rivalry as to who could give away the greatest number of most valuable presents.' [3] The gifts put a seal to marriage, forming a friendly relationship between the two sets of relatives. They give the two sides an identity which is revealed in the taboo which from then on prevents them from visiting or addressing each other, and in the obligation upon them thereafter to make perpetual gift-exchange.[4] The taboo expresses both the intimacy and the fear which arise from this reciprocal creditor-debtor relationship. This is clearly the principle involved since the same taboo, implying simultaneous intimacy and distance, exists between young people of both sexes who have passed through the turtle- and pig-eating ceremonies together,[5] and who are likewise obliged to exchange presents for the rest of their lives. Australia also provides facts of this kind.[6] Radcliffe-Brown mentions rites of reunion—embracing and weeping—and shows how the exchange of presents is the equivalent of this,[7] and how sentiments and persons are mingled.[8] This confusion of personalities and things is precisely the mark of exchange contracts.

2. PRINCIPLES, MOTIVES AND INTENSITY OF GIFT EXCHANGE (MELANESIA)

We saw that the Melanesians have preserved the potlatch better or developed it more highly than the Polynesians. The same is true throughout the whole field of gift-exchange. In Melanesia also the notion of money appears more clearly,[9] and while the system is more complex it is easier to understand.

New Caledonia

In Leenhardt's documents from New Caledonia can be seen the ideas and modes of expression to which we have been drawing attention. His preliminary description of the *pilu-pilu* and the system of feasts, gifts and prestations of all kinds, including money,[10] clearly qualifies them as potlatch. The statements on custom in the formal discourses of the heralds are quite typical. Thus at the start of the ceremonial presentation of yams [11] the herald says: 'If there is some old *pilu* which we have not seen in the country of the Wi . . . this yam will speed there just as formerly such a yam came from thence to us.' [12] Later in the same speech the spirits of the ancestors are said to make the effects of their action and power felt upon the food. 'Today appears the result of the act which you have accomplished. All the generations have appeared in its mouth.' There is another no less graphic way of expressing the link: 'Our feasts are the movement of the needle which sews together the parts of our reed roofs, making of them a single roof, one single word.' [13] The same things (the same thread) return.[14] Other authors have mentioned facts of this kind.[15]

Trobriand Islands

At the other side of the Melanesian world there is a highly evolved system like that of New Caledonia. The Trobrianders are among the most advanced of these peoples. Today as prosperous pearl fishers, and before the arrival of Europeans as flourishing potters and stone workers, they have always been good business men and sturdy sailors. Malinowski compares them with the companions of Jason and names them well the 'Argonauts of the Western Pacific'. In his book of this name, which stands among the best works of descriptive sociology, he treats the subject with which we are concerned, describing the whole system of inter-tribal and intra-tribal commerce known as the *kula*.[16] We still await a full description of their most important institutions, of marriage, funeral ceremonies, initiation, etc., and hence our present remarks are only provisional. But already we have some definite facts of capital importance.[17]

The *kula* is a kind of grand potlatch; it is the vehicle of a great inter-tribal trade extending over all the Trobriands, part of the d'Entrecasteaux group and part of the Amphletts. It has indirect influence on all the tribes and immediate influence on some: Dobu in the Amphletts; Kiriwina, Sinaketa and Kitava in the Trobriands; and Vakuta on Woodlark Island. Malinowski does not translate the word, which probably, however, means 'ring'; and in fact it seems as if all these tribes, the sea journeys, the precious objects, the food and feasts, the economic, ritual and sexual services, the men and the women, were caught in a ring around which they kept up a regular movement in time and space.

Kula trade is aristocratic. It seems to be reserved for the chiefs, who are chiefs of the *kula* fleet and canoes, traders for their vassals (children and brothers-in-law) and, apparently, chiefs over a number of vassal villages. The trade is carried out in noble fashion, disinterestedly and modestly.[18] It is distinguished from the straightforward exchange of useful goods known as the *gimwali*.[19] This is carried on as well as the *kula* in the great primitive fairs which mark inter-tribal *kula* gatherings and in the little *kula* markets of the interior; *gimwali*, however, is distinguished by most tenacious bargaining on both sides, a procedure unworthy of the *kula*. It is said of the individual who does not behave in his *kula* with proper magnanimity that he is conducting it 'as a *gimwali*'. In appearance at any rate, the *kula*, like the American potlatch, consists in giving and receiving,[20] the donors on one occasion being the recipients on the next. Even in the largest, most solemn and highly competitive form of *kula*,[21] that of the great maritime expeditions (*uvalaku*), the rule is to set out with nothing to exchange or even to give in return for food (for which of course it is improper to ask). On these visits one is recipient only, and it is when the visiting tribes the following year become the hosts that gifts are repaid with interest.

With the lesser *kula*, however, the sea voyage also serves as an opportunity for exchange of cargoes; the nobles themselves do business; numerous objects are solicited,[22] demanded and exchanged, and many relationships are established in addition to *kula* ones; but the *kula* remains the most important reason for the expeditions and the relationships set up.

The ceremony of transfer is done with solemnity. The object given is disdained or suspect; it is not accepted until it is thrown on the ground. The donor affects an exaggerated modesty. Solemnly bearing his gift, accompanied by the blowing of a conch-shell, he apologizes for bringing only his leavings and throws the object at his partner's feet.[23] Meanwhile the conch and the herald proclaim to one and all the dignity of the occasion. Pains are taken to show one's freedom and autonomy as well as one's magnanimity,[24] yet all the time one is actuated by the mechanisms of obligation which are resident in the gifts themselves.

The most important things exchanged are *vaygu'a*, a kind of currency.[25] * These are of two sorts: *mwali*, the finely cut and polished armshells worn on great occasions by their owners or relatives, and the *soulava*, necklaces worked by the skilful turners of Sinaketa in handsome red spondylus shell. These are worn by women,[26] and only rarely by men, for example, during sickness. Normally they are hoarded and kept for the joy of having. The manufacture of the one, and the gathering of the other, and the trading of these objects of prestige and exchange form, along with other more common and vulgar pursuits, the source of Trobriand wealth.

According to Malinowski these *vaygu'a* go in a sort of circular movement, the armshells passing regularly from west to east, and the necklaces from east to west.[27] These two opposite movements take place between the d'Entrecasteaux group, the Amphletts, and the isolated islands of Woodlark, Marshall Bennett and Tubetube, and finally the extreme south-east coast of New Guinea, where the unpolished armshells come from. There this trade meets the great expeditions of the same nature from South Massim described by Seligman.[28]

---

* See page 93 for the important note on the principle adopted in discussing the idea of money.

In theory these valuables never stop circulating. It is wrong to keep them too long or to be 'slow' and 'hard' with them; they are passed on only to predetermined partners in the arm-shell or necklace direction.[29] They may be kept from one *kula* to the next while the community gloats over the *vaygu'a* which its chief has obtained. Although there are occasions, such as the preparation of funeral feasts, when it is permitted to receive and to pay nothing,[30] these are no more than a prelude to the feast at which everything is repaid.

The gift received is in fact owned, but the ownership is of a particular kind. One might say that it includes many legal principles which we moderns have isolated from one another. It is at the same time property and a possession, a pledge and a loan, an object sold and an object bought, a deposit, a mandate, a trust; for it is given only on condition that it will be used on behalf of, or transmitted to, a third person, the remote partner (*murimuri*).[31] Such is the economic, legal and moral complex, of quite a typical kind, that Malinowski discovered and described.

This institution also has its mythical, religious and magical aspects. *Vaygu'a* are not indifferent things; they are more than mere coins. All of them, at least the most valuable and most coveted,[32] have a name,[33] a personality, a past, and even a legend attached to them, to such an extent that people may be named after them. One cannot say that they are actually the object of a cult, for the Trobrianders are positivists in their way. But it is impossible not to recognize their superior and sacred nature. To possess one is 'exhilarating, comforting, soothing in itself'.[34] Their owners handle them and gaze at them for hours. Mere contact with them is enough to make them transmit their virtues.[35] You place a *vaygu'a* on the brow or the chest of a sick man, or dangle it before his face. It is his supreme balm.

But more than that, the contract itself partakes of the nature of the *vaygu'a*. Not only armshells and necklaces, but also goods, ornaments, weapons, and everything belonging to the partner, are so alive with feeling, if not with personality, that they have their part in the contract as well.[36] A fine formula, the 'spell of the conch-shell',[37] is used after invoking them to charm or attract towards the partner the things he means to ask and receive.[38] '[A state of excitement [39] seizes my partner.] [40] A state of excitement seizes his dog, his belt, his *gwara* [taboo on cocoanuts and betelnuts],[41] his *bagidou* necklace, his *bagiriku* necklace, his *bagidudu* necklace. . . .' [42]

Another more mythical spell expresses the same idea. The *kula* partner is an animal, a crocodile which he invokes to bring him necklaces.[43]

> 'Crocodile, fall down, take thy man, push him down under the *gebobbo* [part of the canoe where the cargo is stowed]
>
> 'Crocodile, bring me the necklace, bring me the *bagidou*, the *bagiriku*. . . .'

A previous spell in the same ritual invokes a bird of prey.[44]

The last spell of the partners in Dobu or Kitava, by the people of Kiriwina, contains a couplet of which two interpretations are given.[45] The ritual is very long and is repeated many times; its purpose is to enumerate everything forbidden in the *kula*, everything to do with hatred and war which must be conjured away so that trade can take place between friends.

> 'Thy fury, the dog sniffs,
>
> Thy warpaint, the dog sniffs. . . .'

Other versions say:

> 'Thy fury, the dog is docile. . . .'

or:

> 'Thy fury ebbs, it ebbs away, the dog plays about,
>
> Thy anger ebbs. . . .'

This means: 'Thy fury becomes like the dog that plays about.' The point is the metaphor of the dog that rises and licks its master's hand. The Dobuan and his wife should then act in this way. The second interpretation—according to Malinowski somewhat sophisticated and academic, but indigenous all the same—gives a commentary which is more in keeping with what we know already: 'The dogs play nose to nose. When you mention the word dog, the precious objects also come to play.

We have given armshells, and necklaces will come, and they will meet, like dogs which come to sniff.' The expression and metaphor are neat. All the sentiments are seen at once: the possible hatred of the partners, the *vaygu'a* being charmed from their hiding-places; men and precious objects gathering together like dogs that play and run about at the sound of a man's voice.

Another symbolic expression is that of the marriage of armshells, female symbols, with necklaces, male symbols, attracted towards each other like male and female.[46] These various metaphors mean exactly what Maori customary beliefs denote in other terms. Once again it is the confusion of objects, values, contracts and men which finds expression.[47]

Unfortunately we know very little about the sanction behind these transactions. Either it was badly formulated by the people of Kiriwina, Malinowski's informants, or else it is quite clear to the Trobrianders and only needs further research. We have only a few details. The first gift of a *vaygu'a* has the name of *vaga*, opening gift.[48] It definitely binds the recipient to make a return gift, the *yotile*, well translated by Malinowski as the 'clinching gift'.[49] Another name for this is *kudu*, the tooth which bites, severs and liberates.[50] It is obligatory; it is expected and must be equivalent to the first gift; it may be taken by force or surprise.[51] One can avenge non-payment by magic [52] or a show of resentment if the *yotile* does not come up to expectations. If one is unable to repay, one may, if necessary, offer a *basi*, a tooth which does not bite right through but only pierces the skin and leaves the transaction unfinished. It is a temporary affair, the interest on an overdue payment, and although it appeases the creditor it does not absolve the debtor.[53] These details are interesting and the expressions are clear, but the sanction is not at all evident. Is it only mystical and moral? [54] Is the man who is 'hard' in the *kula* only scorned and bewitched? Does not the unfaithful partner lose something else—his rank or at least his position among chiefs? This is something we are not told.

From another angle the institution is typical. Except in old

Germanic custom we have found no system of gift exchange more clear or complete and also better understood both by participants and observer than that described by Malinowski for the Trobrianders.[55]

The *kula* in its essential form is itself only the most solemn part of a vast system of prestations and counter-prestations which seem to embrace the whole social life of the Trobrianders. The *kula* (particularly the inter-island form) appears to be merely the crowning episode of this life. Although it forms one of the great interests of all Trobrianders, and is one of the main reasons for the great expeditions, it is only chiefs, and maritime chiefs at that, who take part in it. The *kula* is the gathering point of many other institutions.

The exchange of *vaygu'a* is set amidst a series of different kinds of exchange, ranging from barter to wage-payment, from solicitation to courtesy, from hospitality to reticence and shame. In the first place, except for the *uvalaku*, the great expeditions of a purely ceremonial and competitive nature, all *kula* transactions are an opportunity for ordinary exchange, *gimwali*, which does not necessarily take place between established partners.[56] Alongside the established partnerships there is an open market between persons of allied tribes. And then between *kula* partners there pass supplementary gifts in an unbroken chain. The *kula* demands them. The association or partnership it sets up and through which it functions starts with a preliminary gift, the *vaga*, which is strenuously sought after by means of solicitory gifts. To obtain this *vaga* a man may flatter his future partner, who is still independent, and to whom he is making a preliminary series of presents.[57] Although one is certain that the *yotile*, the clinching gift, will be returned, one can never say whether the *vaga* will be given in the first place or whether even the solicitory gifts will be accepted. This manner of soliciting and receiving is the rule. Gifts thus made have a special name, in this case *pari*.[58] They are laid out before being presented. Others have names signifying the noble and magical nature of the objects offered.[59] To receive one of these gifts means that one is desirous of entering into and remaining in partnership. Some gifts of this kind have titles which express the legal implications of their acceptance,[60] in which case the affair is considered to be settled. The gift is normally an object of some value, like a large polished stone axe or whalebone knife. To receive it is actually to commit oneself to return the *vaga*, the first desirable gift. But still one is only half a partner. It is the solemn handing over of the *vaga* which finally fixes the partnership. The importance of these gifts arises from the extraordinary competition which exists among members of an expedition. They seek out the best possible partner in the other tribe. For the cause is a great one; the association made establishes a kind of clan link between partners.[61] To get your man you have to seduce him and dazzle him.[62] While paying proper regard to rank,[63] you must get in before the others and make exchanges of the most valuable things—naturally the property of the richest man. The underlying motives are competition, rivalry, show, and a desire for greatness and wealth.[64]

These are the arrival gifts; there are other analogous gifts of departure, called *talo'i* on Sinaketa,[65] and of leave-taking; they are always superior to the gifts of arrival. Here again the cycle of prestations and counter-prestations with interest is accomplished alongside the *kula*.

Naturally at the time of these transactions there are prestations of hospitality, of food, and, on Sinaketa, of women. Finally there are continual supplementary gifts, always regularly repaid. It even seems that these *kortumna* represent a primitive form of the *kula* since they consist of the exchange of stone axes and boars' teeth.[66]

In our view the whole inter-tribal *kula* is an exaggerated case, the most dignified and dramatic example, of a general system. It takes the whole tribe out of the narrow circle of its own frontiers. The same holds also for the clans and villages within the tribes, which are bound by links of the same sort. In this case it is only the local and domestic group and their chiefs which go out to pay visits, do business, and intermarry. Perhaps it is not proper to call this *kula*. Malinowski, however, rightly speaks, in contrast to the maritime *kula*, of the *kula* of the interior and of *kula* communities which provide their chiefs with articles for exchange. It is no exaggeration to speak in these cases of the real potlatch. For instance, the visits of the Kiriwina people to Kitava for mortuary ceremonies (*s'oi*) [67] involve more than the exchange of *vaygu'a*; there is a feigned attack (*youlawada*),[68] a distribution of food, and a display of pigs and yams.

The *vaygu'a* are not always acquired,[69] manufactured,[70] and exchanged by the chiefs in person. Most of them come to the chiefs as gifts from their vassal relatives of inferior rank, particularly brothers-in-law, or from sons with their own fiefs elsewhere.[71] And then on the return of the expedition the *vaygu'a* are solemnly handed over to the village chiefs, the clan chiefs or even to commoners of the clans concerned: in short, to whomsoever has taken part, however indirectly, in the expedition.[72]

Lastly, alongside the internal *kula*, the system of gift-exchange pervades the whole economic life of the Trobriands. Social life is a constant give-and-take; [73] gifts are rendered, received and repaid both obligatorily and in one's own interest, in magnanimity, for repayment of services, or as challenges or pledges. We here set down a few of the most important forms they take.

A relationship analogous to the *kula* is that of the *wasi*.[74] This sets up regular and obligatory exchanges between partners, between agricultural tribes on the one hand and maritime tribes on the other. The agricultural partner places produce in front of the house of his fisherman associate. The latter, after a great fishing expedition, makes return with interest, giving his partner in the agricultural village the product of his catch.[75] Here is the same principle of division of labour as we noticed in New Zealand.

Another remarkable form of exchange takes the form of display.[76] This is *sagali*, a great and frequent distribution of food, made at harvests, during the construction of the chief's house, the building of canoes and funeral ceremonies.[77] The distribution is made to groups that have given their services to the chief or to his clan by means of their crops, or house-beams, or the transport of heavy tree-trunks for canoe-building, or else by services rendered at a funeral by the dead man's clan, and so on.[78] These distributions are in every way similar to the Kwakiutl potlatch, even to the elements of combat and rivalry. Clans and phratries and allied families confront one another and the transactions are group affairs, at least so long as the chief restrains himself.

These group rights and collective economic factors are already some way distant from the *kula*, as are all individual exchange relationships. Some of the latter may be of the order of simple barter. However, since this simple barter takes place only between relatives, close allies or *kula* or *wasi* partners, it hardly seems that exchange even here is really free. Moreover, what one receives, no matter by what means, one may not keep for oneself unless it is quite impossible to do without it. Ordinarily it is passed to someone else, a brother-in-law perhaps.[79] It may happen that the very things which one has received and given away will be returned on the same day.

Returns of prestations of all kinds, of goods or services, fall into the same categories. Here are some presented in no special order.

The *pokala* [80] and *kaributu*,[81] solicitory gifts, which we saw in the *kula*, are species of a much wider genus which corresponds fairly closely to what we know as wages. They are offered to gods and spirits. Another generic name for the same is *vakapula* or *mapula*; [82] these are tokens of recognition and welcome and they too must be repaid. In this regard Malinowski makes what we believe to be an important discovery which explains econo-mic and legal relationships between the sexes in marriage; [83] services of all kinds given to the woman by her husband are con-sidered as a gift-payment for the service the woman renders when she lends him what the Koran calls 'the field'.

The somewhat immature legal language of the Trobrianders has multiplied the names distinguishing all kinds of prestations and counter-prestations according to the name of the prestation repaid,[84] the thing given,[85] the circumstances,[86] and so on. Certain names cover all these considerations: for example, the gift to a magician or for the acquisition of a title is known as *laga*.[87] It is hard to say just how far the vocabulary has been complicated by a strange incapacity for abstraction, and by odd embellishments in the nomenclature.

Other Melanesian Societies

It is unnecessary to multiply the comparisons from many other Melanesian peoples. However, some details may be taken from here and there to strengthen the case and show that the Trobrianders and New Caledonians are not abnormal in having evolved a principle which is strange to other related peoples.

In the extreme south of Melanesia, in Fiji, where we have already identified the potlatch, there are other noteworthy institutions belonging to the gift system. There is a season, the *kerekere*, when it is forbidden to refuse a man anything.[88] Gifts are exchanged between families at marriages, etc.[89] Moreover Fijian money, cachalot teeth, is the same as that of the Trobrianders. It is known as *tambua*. This is supplemented by stones ('mothers' of the teeth), and ornaments, mascots, talismans and lucky charms of the tribe. The sentiments of the Fijians in regard to the *tambua* are the same as those just described: 'They are regarded by their owners very much as a girl regards her dolls. They like to take them out and admire and talk about their beauty; they have a "mother," who is continually being oiled and polished.' Their presentation is a request, and their acceptance a pledge.[90]

The Melanesians of New Guinea and the Papuans influenced by them call their money *tautau*;[91] it is of the same kind and the object of the same beliefs, as that of the Trobriands.[92] We should compare this name with *tahutahu* which means a loan of pigs (Motu and Koita).[93] Now this word is familiar to us as the Polynesian term, the root of the word *taonga* of Samoa and New Zealand—jewels and property incorporated in the family.[94] The words themselves are Polynesian like the objects.[95]

We know that the Melanesians and Papuans of New Guinea have the potlatch.[96]

The fine documentation by Thurnwald on the tribes of Buin [97] and the Banaro [98] have already furnished us with points of comparison. The sacred character of the things exchanged is evident, in particular in the case of money and the way it is given in return for wives, love, songs and services; as in the Trobriands it is a sort of pledge. Thurnwald has analysed too one of the facts which best illustrates this system of reciprocal gifts and the nature of the misnamed 'marriage by purchase'.[99] In reality, this includes prestations from all sides, including the bride's family, and a wife is sent back if her relatives have not offered sufficient gifts in return.

In short this whole island world, and probably also the parts of South-East Asia related to it, reveal similar institutions. Thus the view which we must adopt regarding these Melanesian peoples, who are even wealthier and more commercially inclined than the Polynesians, is very different from the view which is normally taken. They have an extra-domestic economy and a highly developed exchange system, and are busier commercially than French peasants and fishermen have been for the past hundred years. They have an extensive economic life and a considerable trade that cuts across geographical and linguistic boundaries. They replace our system of sale and purchase with one of gifts and return gifts.

In this type of economy, and in the Germanic as we shall see, there is an incapacity to abstract and analyse concepts. But this is unnecessary. In these societies groups cannot analyse themselves or their actions, and influential individuals, however comprehending they may be, do not realize that they *have* to oppose each other. The chief is confounded with his clan and his clan with him, and individuals feel themselves to act only in one way. Holmes makes the acute observation that the Toaripi and Namau languages, the one Papuan and the other Melanesian, which he knew at the mouth of the Finke, have 'only a single word to cover buy and sell, borrow and lend'. Antithetical operations are expressed by the same word. 'Strictly speaking, the natives did not borrow and lend in the manner that we do, but something was always in the form of a honorarium for the loan when it was returned.' [100] These men have neither the notion of selling nor the notion of lending, and yet carry out the legal and economic activities corresponding to these words.

Nor is the notion of barter any more natural to the Melanesians than it is to the Polynesians. Kruyt, one of the better ethnographers, while using the word 'sale', describes exactly this state of mind among the inhabitants of Central Celebes.[101] And yet these Toradja have long been in contact with the Malays who are well known for their trading.

Thus we see that a part of mankind, wealthy, hard-working and creating large surpluses, exchanges vast amounts in ways and for reasons other than those with which we are familiar from our own societies.

3. Honour and Credit (North-West America)

From these observations on Melanesian and Polynesian peoples our picture of gift economy is already beginning to take shape. Material and moral life, as exemplified in gift-exchange, functions there in a manner at once interested and obligatory. Furthermore, the obligation is expressed in myth and imagery, symbolically and collectively; it takes the form of interest in the objects exchanged; the objects are never completely separated from the men who exchange them; the communion and alliance they establish are well-nigh indissoluble. The lasting influence of the objects exchanged is a direct expression of the manner in which sub-groups within segmentary societies of an archaic type are constantly embroiled with and feel themselves in debt to each other.

Indian societies of the American North-West have the same institutions, but in a more radical and accentuated form. Barter is unknown there. Even now after long contact with

Europeans it does not appear that any of the considerable and continual transfers of wealth take place otherwise than through the formality of the potlatch.[102] We now describe this institution as we see it.

First, however, we give a short account of these societies. The tribes in question inhabit the North West American coast —the Tlingit and Haida of Alaska,[103] and the Tsimshian and Kwakiutl of British Columbia.[104] They live on the sea or on the rivers and depend more on fishing than on hunting for their livelihood; but in contrast to the Melanesians and Polynesians they do not practise agriculture. Yet they are very wealthy, and even at the present day their fishing, hunting and trapping activities yield surpluses which are considerable even when reckoned on the European scale. They have the most substantial houses of all the American tribes, and a highly evolved cedar industry. Their canoes are good; and although they seldom venture out on to the open sea they are skilful in navigating around their islands and in coastal waters. They have a high standard of material culture. In particular, even back in the eighteenth century, they collected, smelted, moulded and beat local copper from Tsimshian and Tlingit country. Some of the copper in the form of decorated shields they used as a kind of currency. Almost certainly another form of currency was the beautifully embellished Chilkat blanket-work still used ornamentally, some of it being of considerable value.[105] The peoples are excellent carvers and craftsmen. Their pipes, clubs and sticks are the pride of our ethnological collections. Within broad limits this civilization is remarkably uniform. It is clear that the societies have been in contact with each other from very early days, although their languages suggest that they belong to at least three families of peoples.[106]

Their winter life, even with the southern tribes, is very different from their summer life. The tribes have a two-fold structure: at the end of spring they disperse and go hunting, collect berries from the hillsides and fish the rivers for salmon; while in winter they concentrate in what are known as towns. During this period of concentration they are in a perpetual state of effervescence. The social life becomes intense in the extreme, even more so than in the concentrations of tribes that manage to form in the summer. This life consists of continual movement. There are constant visits of whole tribes to others, of clans to clans and families to families. There is feast upon feast, some of long duration. On the occasion of a marriage, on various ritual occasions, and on social advancement, there is reckless consumption of everything which has been amassed with great industry from some of the richest coasts of the world during the course of summer and autumn. Even private life passes in this manner; clansmen are invited when a seal is killed or a box of roots or berries opened; you invite everyone when a whale runs aground.

Social organization, too, is fairly constant throughout the area though it ranges from the matrilineal phratry (Tlingit and Haida) to the modified matrilineal clan of the Kwakiutl; but the general characters of the social organization and particularly of totemism are repeated in all the tribes. They have associations like those of the Banks Islanders of Melanesia, wrongly called 'secret societies', which are often inter-tribal; and men's and women's societies among the Kwakiutl cut across tribal organization. A part of the gifts and counter-prestations which we shall discuss goes, as in Melanesia,[107] to pay one's way into the successive steps [108] of the associations. Clan and association ritual follows the marriage of chiefs, the sale of coppers, initiations, shamanistic séances and funeral ceremonies, the latter being more particularly pronounced among the Tlingit and Haida. These are all accomplished in the course of an indefinitely prolonged series of potlatches. Potlatches are given in all directions, corresponding to other potlatches to which they are the response. As in Melanesia the process is one of constant give-and-take.

The potlatch, so unique as a phenomenon, yet so typical of these tribes, is really nothing other than gift-exchange.[109] The only differences are in the violence, rivalry and antagonism aroused, in a lack of jural concepts, and in a simpler structure. It is less refined than in Melanesia, especially as regards the northern tribes, the Tlingit and the Haida,[110] but the collective nature of the contract is more pronounced than in Melanesia and Polynesia.[111] Despite appearances, the institutions here are nearer to what we call simple total prestations. Thus the legal and economic concepts attached to them have less clarity and conscious precision. Nevertheless, in action the principles emerge formally and clearly.

There are two traits more in evidence here than in the Melanesian potlatch or in the more evolved and discrete institutions of Polynesia: the themes of credit and honour.[112]

As we have seen, when gifts circulate in Melanesia and Polynesia the return is assured by the virtue of the things passed on, which are their own guarantees. In any society it is in the nature of the gift in the end to being its own reward. By definition, a common meal, a distribution of *kava*, or a charm worn, cannot be repaid at once. Time has to pass before a counter-prestation can be made. Thus the notion of time is logically implied when one pays a visit, contracts a marriage or an alliance, makes a treaty, goes to organized games, fights or feasts of others, renders ritual and honorific service and 'shows respect', to use the Tlingit term.[113] All these are things exchanged side by side with other material objects, and they are the more numerous as the society is wealthier.

On this point, legal and economic theory is greatly at fault. Imbued with modern ideas, current theory tends towards *a priori* notions of evolution,[114] and claims to follow a so-called necessary logic; in fact, however, it remains based on old traditions. Nothing could be more dangerous than what Simiand called this 'unconscious sociology'. For instance, Cuq could still say in 1910: 'In primitive societies barter alone is found; in those more advanced, direct sale is practised. Sale on credit characterizes a higher stage of civilization; it appears first in an indirect manner, a combination of sale and loan.' [115] In fact the origin of credit is different. It is to be found in a range of customs neglected by lawyers and economists as uninteresting: namely the gift, which is a complex phenomenon especially in its ancient form of total prestation, which we are studying here. Now a gift necessarily implies the notion of credit. Economic evolution has not gone from barter to sale and from cash to credit. Barter arose from the system of gifts given and received on credit, simplified by drawing together the moments of time which had previously been distinct. Likewise purchase and sale—both direct sale and credit sale— and the loan, derive from the same source. There is nothing to suggest that any economic system which has passed through the phase we are describing was ignorant of the idea of credit, of which all archaic societies around us are aware. This is a simple and realistic manner of dealing with the problem, which Davy has already studied, of the 'two moments of time' which the contract unites.[116]

No less important is the role which honour plays in the transactions of the Indians. Nowhere else is the prestige of an individual as closely bound up with expenditure, and with the duty of returning with interest gifts received in such a way that the creditor becomes the debtor. Consumption and destruction are virtually unlimited. In some potlatch systems one is constrained to expend everything one possesses and to keep nothing.[117] The rich man who shows his wealth by spending recklessly is the man who wins prestige. The principles of rivalry and antagonism are basic. Political and individual status in associations and clans, and rank of every kind, are determined by the war of property, as well as by armed hostilities, by chance, inheritance, alliance or marriage.[118] But everything is conceived as if it were a war of wealth.[119] Marriage of one's children and one's position at gatherings are determined solely in the course of the potlatch given and returned. Position is also lost as in war, gambling,[120] hunting and wrestling.[121] Sometimes there is no question of receiving return; one destroys simply in order to give the appearance that one has no desire to receive anything back.[122] Whole cases of candle-fish or whale oil,[123] houses, and blankets by the thousand are burnt; the most valuable coppers are broken and thrown into the sea to level and crush a rival. Progress up the social ladder is made in this way not only for oneself but also for one's family. Thus in a system of this kind much wealth is continually being consumed and transferred. Such transfers may if desired be called exchange or even commerce or sale; [124] but it is an aristocratic type of commerce characterized by etiquette and generosity; moreover, when it is carried out in a different spirit, for immediate gain, it is viewed with the greatest disdain. [125]

We see, then, that the notion of honour, strong in Polynesia, and present in Melanesia, is exceptionally marked here. On this point the classical writings made a poor estimate of the motives which animate men and of all that we owe to societies that preceded our own. Even as informed a scholar as Huvelin felt obliged to deduce the notion of honour—which is reputedly *without* efficacy—from the notion of magical efficacy. [126] The truth is more complex. The notion of honour is no more foreign to these civilizations than the notion of magic. [127] Polynesian *mana* itself symbolizes not only the magical power of the person but also his honour, and one of the best translations of the word is 'authority' or 'wealth'. [128] The Tlingit or Haida potlatch consists in considering mutual services as honours. [129] Even in really primitive societies like the Australian, the 'point of honour' is as ticklish as it is in ours; and it may be satisfied by prestations, offerings of food, by precedence or ritual, as well as by gifts. [130] Men could pledge their honour long before they could sign their names.

The North-West American potlatch has been studied enough as to the form of the contract. But we must find a place for the researches of Davy and Adam in the wider framework of our subject. For the potlatch is more than a legal phenomenon; it is one of those phenomena we propose to call 'total'. It is religious, mythological and shamanistic because the chiefs taking part are incarnations of gods and ancestors, whose names they bear, whose dances they dance and whose spirits possess them. [131] It is economic; and one has to assess the value, importance, causes and effects of transactions which are enormous even when reckoned by European standards. The potlatch is also a phenomenon of social morphology; the reunion of tribes, clans, families and nations produces great excitement. People fraternize but at the same time remain strangers; community of interest and opposition are revealed constantly in a great whirl of business.[132] Finally, from the jural point of view, we have already noted the contractual forms and what we might call the human element of the contract, and the legal status of the contracting parties—as clans or families or with reference to rank or marital condition; and to this we now add that the material objects of the contracts have a virtue of their own which causes them to be given and compels the making of counter-gifts.

It would have been useful, if space had been available, to distinguish four forms of American potlatch: first, potlatch where the phratries and chiefs' families alone take part (Tlingit); second, potlatches in which phratries, clans, families and chiefs take more or less similar roles (Haida); third, potlatch with chiefs and their clans confronting each other (Tsimshian); and fourth, potlatch of chiefs and fraternities (Kwakiutl). But this would prolong our argument, and in any case three of the four forms (with the exception of the Tsimshian) have already been comparatively described by Davy.[133] But as far as our study is concerned all the forms are more or less identical as regards the elements of the gift, the obligation to receive and the obligation to make a return.

4. THE THREE OBLIGATIONS: GIVING, RECEIVING, REPAYING

The Obligation to Give

This is the essence of potlatch. A chief must give a potlatch for himself, his son, his son-in-law or daughter [134] and for the dead.[135] He can keep his authority in his tribe, village and family, and maintain his position with the chiefs inside and outside his nation,[136] only if he can prove that he is favourably regarded by the spirits, that he possesses fortune [137] and that he is possessed by it.[138] The only way to demonstrate his fortune is by expending it to the humiliation of others, by putting them

'in the shadow of his name'.[139] Kwakiutl and Haida noblemen
have the same notion of 'face' as the Chinese mandarin or
officer.[140] It is said of one of the great mythical chiefs who gave
no feast that he had a 'rotten face'.[141] The expression is more
apt than it is even in China; for to lose one's face is to lose one's
spirit, which is truly the 'face', the dancing mask, the right to
incarnate a spirit and wear an emblem or totem. It is the
veritable *persona* which is at stake, and it can be lost in the
potlatch [142] just as it can be lost in the game of gift-giving,[143] in
war,[144] or through some error in ritual.[145] In all these societies
one is anxious to give; there is no occasion of importance (even
outside the solemn winter gatherings) when one is *not* obliged
to invite friends to share the produce of the chase or the forest
which the gods or totems have sent; [146] to redistribute everything received at a potlatch; or to recognize services [147] from
chiefs, vassals or relatives [148] by means of gifts. Failing these
obligations—at least for the nobles—etiquette is violated and
rank is lost.[149]

The obligation to invite is particularly evident between
clans or between tribes. It makes sense only if the invitation is
given to people other than members of the family, clan or
phratry.[150] Everyone who can, will or does attend the potlatch
must be invited.[151] Neglect has fateful results.[152] An important
Tsimshian myth [153] shows the state of mind in which the central
theme of much European folklore originated: the myth of the
bad fairy neglected at a baptism or marriage. Here the institutional fabric in which it is sewn appears clearly, and we realize
the kind of civilization in which it functioned. A princess of one
of the Tsimshian villages conceives in the 'Country of the
Otters' and gives birth miraculously to 'Little Otter'. She
returns with her child to the village of her father, the chief.
Little Otter catches halibut with which her father feeds all the
tribal chiefs. He introduces Little Otter to everyone and
requests them not to kill him if they find him fishing in his
animal form: 'Here is my grandson who has brought for you
this food with which I serve you, my guests.' Thus the grandfather grows rich with all manner of wealth brought to him by

the chiefs when they come in the winter hunger to eat whale and seal and the fresh fish caught by Little Otter. But one chief is not invited. And one day when the crew of a canoe of the neglected tribe meets Little Otter at sea the bowman kills him and takes the seal. The grandfather and all the tribes search high and low for Little Otter until they hear about the neglected tribe. The latter offers its excuses; it has never heard of Little Otter. The princess dies of grief; the involuntarily guilty chief brings the grandfather all sorts of gifts in expiation. The myth ends: 'That is why the people have great feasts when a chief's son is born and gets a name; for none may be ignorant of him.' [154] The potlatch—the distribution of goods—is the fundamental act of public recognition in all spheres, military, legal, economic and religious. The chief or his son is recognized and acknowledged by the people.[155]

Sometimes the ritual in the feasts of the Kwakiutl and other tribes in the same group expresses this obligation to invite.[156] Part of the ceremonial opens with the 'ceremony of the dogs'. These are represented by masked men who come out of one house and force their way into another. They commemorate the occasion on which the people of the three other tribes of Kwakiutl proper neglected to invite the clan which ranked highest among them, the Guetela who, having no desire to remain outsiders, entered the dancing house and destroyed everything.[157]

The Obligation to Receive

This is no less constraining. One does not have the right to refuse a gift or a potlatch.[158] To do so would show fear of having to repay, and of being abased in default. One would 'lose the weight' of one's name by admitting defeat in advance.[159] In certain circumstances, however, a refusal can be an assertion of victory and invincibility.[160] It appears at least with the Kwakiutl that a recognized position in the hierarchy, or a victory through previous potlatches, allows one to refuse an invitation or even a gift without war ensuing. If this is so, then a potlatch must be carried out by the man who refuses to accept the invitation. More particularly, he has to contribute to the 'fat festival' in which a ritual of refusal may be observed.[161] The chief who considers himself superior refuses the spoonful of fat offered him: he fetches his copper and returns with it to 'extinguish the fire' (of the fat). A series of formalities follow which mark the challenge and oblige the chief who has refused to give another potlatch or fat festival.[162] In principle, however, gifts are always accepted and praised.[163] You must speak your appreciation of food prepared for you.[164] But you accept a challenge at the same time.[165] You receive a gift 'on the back'. You accept the food and you do so because you mean to take up the challenge and prove that you are not unworthy.[166] When chiefs confront each other in this manner they may find themselves in odd situations and probably they experience them as such. In like manner in ancient Gaul and Germany, as well as nowadays in gatherings of French farmers and students, one is pledged to swallow quantities of liquid to 'do honour' in grotesque fashion to the host. The obligation stands even although one is only heir to the man who bears the challenge.[167] Failure to give or receive,[168] like failure to make return gifts, means a loss of dignity.[169]

The Obligation to Repay

Outside pure destruction the obligation to repay is the essence of potlatch.[170] Destruction is very often sacrificial, directed towards the spirits, and apparently does not require a return unconditionally, especially when it is the work of a superior clan chief or of the chief of a clan already recognized as superior.[171] But normally the potlatch must be returned with interest like all other gifts. The interest is generally between 30 and 100 per cent. a year. If a subject receives a blanket from his chief for a service rendered he will return two on the occasion of a marriage in the chief's family or on the initiation of the chief's son. But then the chief in his turn redistributes to him whatever he gets from the next potlatch at which rival clans repay the chief's generosity.

The obligation of worthy return is imperative.[172] Face is lost for ever if it is not made or if equivalent value is not destroyed.[173]

The sanction for the obligation to repay is enslavement for debt. This is so at least for the Kwakiutl, Haida and Tsimshian. It is an institution comparable in nature and function to the Roman *nexum*. The person who cannot return a loan or potlatch loses his rank and even his status of a free man. If among the Kwakiutl a man of poor credit has to borrow he is said to 'sell a slave'. We need not stress the similarity of this expression with the Roman one.[174] The Haida say, as if they had invented the Latin phrase independently, that a girl's mother who gives a betrothal payment to the mother of a young chief 'puts a thread on him'.

Just as the Trobriand *kula* is an extreme case of gift exchange, so the potlatch in North-West America is the monster child of the gift system. In societies of phratries, amongst the Tlingit and Haida, we find important traces of a former total prestation (which is characteristic of the Athabascans, a related group). Presents are exchanged on any pretext for any service, and everything is returned sooner or later for redistribution.[175] The Tsimshian have almost the same rules.[176] Among the Kwakiutl these rules, in many cases, function outside the potlatch.[177] We shall not press this obvious point; old authors described the potlatch in such a way as to make it doubtful whether it was or was not a distinct institution.[178] We may recall that with the Chinook, one of the least known tribes but one which would repay study, the word 'potlatch' means 'gift'.[179]

5. THE POWER IN OBJECTS OF EXCHANGE

Our analysis can be carried farther to show that in the things exchanged at a potlatch there is a certain power which forces them to circulate, to be given away and repaid.

To begin with, the Kwakiutl and Tsimshian, and perhaps others, make the same distinction between the various types of property as do the Romans, Trobrianders and Samoans. They have the ordinary articles of consumption and distribution and perhaps also of sale (I have found no trace of barter). They have also the valuable family property—talismans, decorated coppers, skin blankets and embroidered fabrics.[180] This class of articles is transmitted with that solemnity with which women are given in marriage, privileges are endowed on sons-in-law, and names and status are given to children and daughters' husbands.[181] It is wrong to speak here of alienation, for these things are loaned rather than sold and ceded. Basically they are *sacra* which the family parts with, if at all, only with reluctance.

Closer observation reveals similar distinctions among the Haida. This tribe has in fact sacralized, in the manner of Antiquity, the notions of property and wealth. By a religious and mythological effort of a type rare enough in the Americas they have managed to reify an abstraction: the 'Property Woman', of whom we possess myths and a description.[182] She is nothing less than the mother, the founding goddess of the dominant phratry, the Eagles. But oddly enough—a fact which recalls the Asiatic world and Antiquity—she appears identical with the 'queen', the principal piece in the game of tip-cat, the piece that wins everything and whose name the Property Woman bears. This goddess is found in Tlingit [183] country and her myth, if not her cult, among the Tsimshian [184] and Kwakiutl.[185]

Together these precious family articles constitute what one might call the magical legacy of the people; they are conceived as such by their owner, by the initiate he gives them to, by the ancestor who endowed the clan with them, and by the founding hero of the clan to whom the spirits gave them.[186] In any case in all these clans they are spiritual in origin and nature.[187] Further, they are kept in a large ornate box which itself is endowed with a powerful personality, which speaks, is in communion with the owner, contains his soul, and so on.[188]

Each of these precious objects and tokens of wealth has, as amongst the Trobrianders, its name,[189] quality and power.[190]

The large *abalone* shells,[191] the shields covered with them, the decorated blankets with faces, eyes, and animal and human figures embroidered and woven into them, are all personalities.[192] The houses and decorated beams are themselves beings.[193] Everything speaks—roof, fire, carvings and paintings; for the magical house is built not only by the chief and his people and those of the opposing phratry but also by the gods and ancestors; spirits and young initiates are welcomed and cast out by the house in person.[194]

Each of these precious things has, moreover, a productive capacity within it.[195] Each, as well as being a sign and surety of life, is also a sign and surety of wealth, a magico-religious guarantee of rank and prosperity.[196] Ceremonial dishes and spoons decorated and carved with the clan totem or sign of rank, are animate things.[197] They are replicas of the never-ending supply of tools, the creators of food, which the spirits gave to the ancestors. They are supposedly miraculous. Objects are confounded with the spirits who made them, and eating utensils with food. Thus Kwakiutl dishes and Haida spoons are essential goods with a strict circulation and are carefully shared out between the families and clans of the chiefs.

6. 'MONEY OF RENOWN' (RENOMMIERGELD) [198]

Decorated coppers[199] are the most important articles in the potlatch, and beliefs and a cult are attached to them. With all these tribes copper, a living being, is the object of cult and myth.[200] Copper, with the Haida and Kwakiutl at least, is identified with salmon, itself an object of cult.[201] But in addition to this mythical element each copper is by itself an object of individual beliefs.[202] Each principal copper of the families of clan chiefs has its name and individuality;[203] it has also its own value,[204] in the full magical and economic sense of the word, which is regulated by the vicissitudes of the potlatches through which it passes and even by its partial or complete destruction.[205]

Coppers have also a virtue which attracts other coppers to them, as wealth attracts wealth and as dignity attracts honours, spirit-possession and good alliances.[206] In this way they live their own lives and attract other coppers.[207] One of the Kwakiutl coppers is called 'Bringer of Coppers' and the formula describes how the coppers gather around it, while the name of its owner is 'Copper-Flowing-Towards-Me'.[208] With the Haida and Tlingit, coppers are a 'fortress' for the princess who owns them; elsewhere a chief who owns them is rendered invincible.[209] They are the 'flat divine objects' of the house.[210] Often the myth identifies together the spirits who gave the coppers, the owners and the coppers themselves.[211] It is impossible to discern what makes the power of the one out of the spirit and the wealth of the other; a copper talks and grunts, demanding to be given away or destroyed; [212] it is covered with blankets to keep it warm just as a chief is smothered in the blankets he is to distribute.[213]

From another angle we see the transmission of wealth and good fortune.[214] The spirits and minor spirits of an initiate allow him to own coppers and talismans which then enable him to acquire other coppers, greater wealth, higher rank and more spirits (all of these being equivalents). If we consider the coppers with other forms of wealth which are the object of hoarding and potlatch—masks, talismans and so on—we find they are all confounded in their uses and effects.[215] Through them rank is obtained; because a man obtains wealth he obtains a spirit which in turn possesses him, enabling him to overcome obstacles heroically. Then later the hero is paid for his shamanistic services, ritual dances and trances. Everything is tied together; things have personality, and personalities are in some manner the permanent possession of the clan. Titles, talismans, coppers and spirits of chiefs are homonyms and synonyms, having the same nature and function.[216] The circulation of goods follows that of men, women and children, of festival ritual, ceremonies and dances, jokes and injuries. Basically they are the same. If things are given and returned it is precisely because one gives and returns 'respects' and 'courtesies'. But in addition, in giving them, a man gives himself, and he does so because he owes himself—himself and his possessions—to others.

7. PRIMARY CONCLUSION

From our study of four important groups of people we find the following: first, in two or three of the groups, we find the potlatch, its leading motive and its typical form. In all groups we see the archaic form of exchange—the gift and the return gift. Moreover, in these societies we note the circulation of objects side by side with the circulation of persons and rights. We might stop at this point. The amount, distribution and importance of our data authorize us to conceive of a régime embracing a large part of humanity over a long transitional phase, and persisting to this day among peoples other than those described. We may then consider that the spirit of gift-exchange is characteristic of societies which have passed the phase of 'total prestation' (between clan and clan, family and family) but have not yet reached the stage of pure individual contract, the money market, sale proper, fixed price, and weighed and coined money.

CHAPTER III

SURVIVALS IN EARLY LITERATURE

T HE preceding data come from the domain of ethnography, and are all drawn from societies bordering the Pacific. It is usual for facts of this sort to be treated as curiosities, or to be used to show, by comparison, how far our own institutions approach them or differ from them. Nevertheless, they have a sociological significance since they lead us towards the understanding of a stage in social evolution. They also have a bearing on social history, for institutions of this type are a step in the development of our own economic forms, and serve as a historical explanation of features of our own society. We may also find that exchange in the societies which immediately preceded our own reveals important traces of the moral and economic principles we have just analysed for primitive societies. We believe we can demonstrate that our own economic institutions have arisen from ones of the type we have just reviewed.[1]

We live in a society where there is a marked distinction (although nowadays the distinction is criticized by lawyers themselves) between real and personal law, between things and persons. This distinction is fundamental; it is the very condition of part of our system of property, alienation and exchange. Yet it is foreign to the customs we have been studying. Likewise Greek, Roman and Semitic civilizations distinguished clearly between obligatory prestations and pure gifts. But are these distinctions not of relatively recent appearance in the codes of the great civilizations? Did not those civilizations pass through a previous phase in which their thought was less cold and calculating? Did not they themselves at one time practise these customs of gift-exchange in which persons and things become indistinguishable? Analysis of some aspects of Indo-European law shows clearly that usage has in fact changed in this way. We find traces of the transformation in Rome. In India and Germany we see that institutions of this primitive type were functioning at a fairly recent date.

1. Personal Law and Real Law (Ancient Rome)

A comparison of archaic custom with Roman custom prior to the historic era [2] and Germanic custom of the period when it enters history sheds light upon the law of persons and the law of things. In particular it allows us to reconsider one of the most controversial questions of legal history, the theory of the *nexum*.[3]

Huvelin profitably compares *nexum* with the Germanic *wadium* and more generally with the other supplementary sureties given during the course of a contract; and then compares the sureties with sympathetic magic and the power which a thing, once in contact with a man, gives to his contracting partner.[4] This explains only some of the data. A magical sanction remains merely a possibility and depends on the nature and character of the object given. The supplementary surety and the Germanic *wadium* are not simply exchanges of sureties or warrants endowed with some mystical superiority.[5] The thing pledged is normally of little value—a stick, the Roman *stips*,[6] or the Germanic *festuca notata;* even the *arrhes* (earnest) of Semitic origin is something more than an advance payment.[7] These are live things. Probably they are to be considered as survivals of older obligatory gifts or reciprocal dues. The contracting parties are bound by them. In this respect these supplementary exchanges are fictitious expressions of the movement of personalities and the objects confounded with them. The *nexum*, the legal bond, derives from things as well as from men.[8]

The formality with which they were exchanged is proof of their importance. In quiritary Roman law, property (essential property consisting of slaves and cattle and later of real estate) was never handed over in an easy or informal manner. The

transaction was always a solemn affair, made before five
witnesses or friends and the 'weigher'.[9] It was tied up with all
manner of considerations foreign to our modern conceptions
with their purely legal and economic elements. The *nexum*
established still involved religious representations (which
Huvelin saw but considered to be exclusively magical).

Certainly the oldest form of contract in Roman law, the
nexum, is already distinct from the collective contract and the
old system of binding gifts. The early history of the Roman
system of obligations may never be written with any certainty.
Nevertheless it is possible to point out how research on this
matter might proceed.

We hold that there is a connecting bond in things other
than the magical and religious one—a bond created by the
words and gestures of legal formalism. This bond is strongly
marked in certain very old terms in Roman and Italic law.
The etymology of a number of these words is suggestive. What
follows here is in the nature of a hypothesis.

Originally, we contend, things had a personality and a
virtue of their own. Things are not the inert objects which the
laws of Justinian and ourselves imply. They are a part of the
family: the Roman *familia* comprises the *res* as well as the
personae.[10] It is defined in the *Digest*, and we note that the farther
back we go into Antiquity the more the *familia* denotes the *res*
of which it consists even to the family's food and means of
livelihood.[11] The best etymology of the word *familia* is that
which aligns it with the Sanskrit *dhaman*, a house.[12]

Things were of two kinds. Distinction was made between
familia and *pecunia*, between the things of the house (slaves,
horses, mules, donkeys) and the cattle in the fields far from the
stables.[13] There was also a distinction between *res mancipi* and
res nec mancipi according to the manner in which they were sold.[14]
With the former, which constituted objects of value, including
children and real estate, alienation had to follow the form of
mancipatio, 'taking into the hands'.[15] There is still discussion
whether the distinction between *familia* and *pecunia* coincided
with that between *res mancipi* and *res nec mancipi*. It seems to us

that there is not the slightest doubt that at least originally they did coincide. The things that escaped the *mancipatio* were precisely the cattle and *pecunia*, money, the idea, name and form of which derived from cattle. One might say that the Roman *veteres* made the same distinction as the Tsimshian and Kwakiutl do between the permanent and essential goods of the house, and the things that pass on—food, beasts in the distant grazing, and metals—in which the unemancipated son might trade.

Moreover, the *res* cannot originally have been the brute and tangible thing, the simple and passive object of transaction that it has become. The best etymology seems to be that which compares the word with the Sanskrit *rah*, *ratih*, meaning a gift or pleasant thing.[16] The *res* must originally have meant that which gives a person pleasure.[17] Moreover, the thing was always marked with a family seal or property mark. Hence we can understand that with things *mancipi* the solemn act of *mancipatio* created a legal bond. For even in the hands of the *accipiens* it still remained a factor in the family of the original owner; it remained bound to that family and likewise bound to the latest owner until he was freed by the fulfilment of his part of the contract, that is to say by the transmission of the compensating article, price or service which in its turn was binding on the original owner.

In respect of two points of Roman law, theft (*furtum*) and contracts *re*, the idea of the power inherent in a thing was always present. As far as theft is concerned, the acts and obligations to which it gave rise were clearly due to this power.[18] It had *aeterna auctoritas* which made its presence felt if it was stolen.[19] In this respect the *res* of Roman law was no different from Hindu or Haida property.[20] Contracts *re* consisted of four of the most important contracts in law: loan, deposit, pledge and free loan. A certain number of other contracts, in particular gift and exchange, which we consider with sale to have been the original kinds of contract, were also taken to be contracts *re*.[21] But in fact, even in our own laws, it is not possible to forget the older forms.[22] For a gift to be made, there must be presupposed an object or service which creates an obligation. It is clear, for instance, that the revocability of a gift as a result of ingratitude, which came late in Roman law [23] but was always present in ours, is a normal, perhaps even natural legal institution.

These facts, though, are not of wide occurrence and we want our study to be general. We believe that in ancient Rome the act of *traditio* of a *res*, and not only the words or writing about it, was one of the essential factors. Roman law itself never made this clear. For although it proclaimed that the solemnity of the occasion was essential—just as is the case in the archaic customs we have described—saying *nunquam nuda traditio transfert dominium*,[24] it maintained at the same time, as late as Diocletian (298 B.C.): *Traditionibus et usucapionibus dominia, non pactis transferentur.*[25] The *res*, prestation or article is an essential element in the contract. We are ill placed to resolve these much-debated etymological problems of concepts in view of the poverty of the sources.

Up to this point we feel sure of our facts. If we push farther and indicate to lawyers and philologists what might be a fruitful line of research, it may be possible to discern a legal system in force before the time of the Twelve Tables. It is not only *familia* and *res* which are open to analysis. We put forward a number of hypotheses, each of which taken alone carries little weight, but which, when considered together, may be found to have some significance.

Most expressions of contract and obligation and some of the forms of contract seem to be referable to the system of spiritual bonds created by the act of *traditio*.

The contracting party is first *reus;* he is originally the man who has received the *res* from another and who becomes the *reus*—that is, bound to him by virtue of the thing alone, or by its spirit.[26] Hirn suggested an etymology which has been considered meaningless, although its meaning is clear. As he points out, *reus* was originally a genitive ending in *-os*, and replaces *rei-jos*, the man who is possessed by the thing.[27] It is true that Hirn, and Walde who follows him,[28] translate *res* by 'legal action', and *rei-jos* as 'implicated in a legal action'.[29] But this is arbitrary and presupposes that *res* means legal action. On the contrary, if our derivation is accepted, every *res* and every *traditio* of *res* being the object of a legal action in public, it becomes clear that 'implicated in a legal action' is merely a derived meaning. Thus the meaning of 'guilty' for *reus* is even farther derived. Thus we should prefer to say that the word meant first the person possessed by the thing, then the person implicated in the legal action arising out of the *traditio* of the thing, and finally the guilty and responsible person. From this point of view all the theories of the quasi-delict origin of contract, *nexum* and *actio* are slightly illuminated. The mere fact of having the thing puts the *accipiens* in a condition of quasi-culpability (*damnatus, nexus, aere obseratus*), of spiritual inferiority, moral inequality (*magister, minister*) vis-à-vis the donor, the *tradens*.[30]

We refer now to a number of very old traits connected with *mancipatio*,[31] the purchase and sale which became the *emptio venditio* of very ancient Roman law.[32] We note first that this always implies *traditio*.[33] The first holder, *tradens*, shows his property, detaches himself from it, hands it over and thus buys the *accipiens*. True *mancipatio* corresponds to this operation. The person who receives the thing takes it into his hands. He does not merely recognize that he has received it, but realizes that he himself is 'bought' until it is paid for. Normally only one *mancipatio* is considered, and it is understood to be simply the act of taking into possession, but in the one operation many others of the same nature are included concerning both things and persons.

There is much discussion also on the *emptio venditio*.[34] Does it correspond to two acts or one? We adduce a reason why two acts should be counted although in a direct sale they may follow right on top of each other. Just as in primitive custom we find the gift followed by the return gift, so in Roman usage there is sale and then payment. In this way there is no difficulty in understanding the whole process, including the stipulation.[35]

It is sufficient merely to note the formulae used—that of

the *mancipatio* concerning the piece of bronze, and that of the acceptance of the money of the slave who redeems himself (this money must be '*puri, probi, profani sui*').[36] These two forms are identical. Both also are echoes of the formulae for the older *emptio* of cattle and slaves preserved for us in the *jus civile*.[37] The second holder accepts the thing only when it is free of vice; and he accepts it only because he is in a position to return something, to compensate, to pay the price. Note the expressions: *reddit pretium*, *reddere*, etc., where the root *dare* still appears.[38]

Festus has preserved for us the meaning of the term *emere* (to buy), and of the form of civil law it implies. He says: '*Abemito significat demito vel auferto; emere enim antiqui dicebant pro accipere.*' and also: '*Emere quod nunc est mercari antiqui accipiebant pro sumere.*' This is the meaning of the Indo-European word which is connected with the Latin one. *Emere* is to take or accept something from a person.[39]

The term *emptio venditio* seems to suggest laws other than Roman,[40] for which, in the absence of money and price, there was only barter and gift. *Vendere*, originally *venum dare*, is a composite word of an archaic or even prehistoric type.[41] There is no doubt that it contains the element *dare*, which implies gift and transmission. For the other element we borrow an Indo-European word implying not sale but the price of sale, ὠνή, Sanskrit *vasnah*, which Hirn compares with a Bulgarian word signifying dowry, the purchase price of a woman.[42]

These hypotheses about very ancient Roman law are of rather a prehistoric order. The law, morality and economy of the Latins must have had these forms, but they were forgotten when the institutions approached the historic era. For it was precisely these Greeks and Romans who, possibly following the Northern and Western Semites, drew the distinction between ritual, law and economic interest.[43] By a venerable revolution they passed beyond that antiquated and dangerous gift economy, encumbered by personal considerations, incompatible with the development of the market, trade and productivity—which was in a word uneconomic.

Our reconstruction is nothing more than a likely hypothesis, but its degree of probability increases with the fact that other trustworthy Indo-European written laws were witness in historic times to a system of the kind already described among Pacific and American societies which, although we call them 'primitive', are at least 'archaic'. Thus we can generalize with some degree of safety. The two Indo-European systems which have best conserved these traces are the Germanic and the Hindu. They also happen to be those on which we have the most complete texts.

2. THEORY OF THE GIFT (HINDU CLASSICAL PERIOD) [44]

There is a serious difficulty in the use of Hindu legal documents. The codes, and the epics which equal them in authority, were written by Brahmins, if not for themselves at least to their advantage, at the period of their triumph.[45] They give us only theoretical law. Thus we can discover data about the other castes, Ksatriya and Vaicya, only by making reconstructions from the numerous unconnected statements about them in the literature. The theory of *danadharma*, the 'law of the gift', which we shall discuss, applies only to Brahmins; for instance, how they solicit and receive then make return wholly by religious services. It shows also the way in which gifts are due to them. Naturally this duty of giving to the Brahmins is subject to numerous prescriptions. It is probable that entirely different relationships obtained among noblemen, princely families and the numerous castes and races of the common people. It would be a difficult matter to assess them on account of the nature of our Hindu data.

Ancient India immediately after the Aryan invasion was in two respects a land of the potlatch.[46] This was still found among two large groups which had once been more numerous and which now formed the substratum of a great part of the population: the Tibeto-Burmans of Assam and the tribes of Munda stock, the Austro-Asiatics. We may even suppose that the traditions of these tribes have persisted in a Brahminic setting.[47] For instance, traces may be seen of an institution, comparable with the Batak *indjok* and other features of Malayan hospitality, in the rules which forbid eating with an uninvited guest. Institutions of the same genus if not of the same species have left their traces in the oldest *Veda*, and they are nearly all found again in the Indo-European world.[48] Thus there are reasons for believing that the Aryans also had them in India.[49] The two currents flowed together at a time which can be fairly accurately assessed, contemporary with the later parts of the *Veda* and the colonization of the two great river plains of the Indus and Ganges. No doubt the two currents reinforced each other. Thus as soon as we leave the Vedic period of the literature we find the theory strongly developed. The *Mahabharata* is the story of a tremendous potlatch—there is a game of dice between the Kauravas and the Pandavas, and a military festival, while Draupadi, sister and polyandrous wife of the Pandavas, chooses husbands.[50] Repetitions of the same cycle of legends are met with in the finest parts of the epics; for instance, the tale of Nala and Damayanyi, like the *Mahabharata*, recounts communal house-building, a game of dice and so on.[51] But the whole is disfigured by its literary and theological style.

For our present demonstration it is not necessary to weigh up these multiple origins and make a hypothetical reconstruction of the whole system.[52] Likewise the number of castes that were concerned and the exact period at which they flourished are irrelevant in a work of comparison. Later, for reasons which need not concern us here, this law disappeared except among the Brahmins; but we can say for sure that it functioned between the eighth century B.C. and the second or third century A.D. That is precise enough for our purpose. The epics and laws of the Brahmins move in the old atmosphere in which gifts are still obligatory and have special virtues and form a part of human persons. We limit ourselves here to a description of these forms of social life and a study of their causes.

The thing given brings return in this life and in the other.

It may automatically bring the donor an equivalent return—it is not lost to him, but reproductive; or else the donor finds the thing itself again, but with increase.[53] Food given away means that food will return to the donor in this world; it also means food for him in the other world and in his series of reincarnations. Water, wells and springs given away are insurance against thirst; the clothes, the sunshades, the gold, the sandals for protection against the burning earth, return to you in this life and in the other.[54] The land you give away produces crops for another person and enhances your own interests in both worlds and in future incarnations. 'As the crescent moon grows from day to day so the gift of land once made increases at every harvest.' Land gives crops, rents and taxes, minerals and cattle. A gift made of it enriches both donor and recipient with the same produce.[55] Such economic theology is developed at great length in the rolling periods of the innumerable cantos, and neither the codes nor the epics ever tire of the subject.[56]

Land, food, or whatever one gives away are, moreover, personified beings that talk and take part in the contract. They state their desire to be given away. The land once spoke to the sun hero Rama, son of Jamadagni, and when he heard its song he gave it over to the *rsi* Kacyapa. The land said to him, in its no doubt old-fashioned language:

> 'Receive me [to the recipient]
> Give me [to the donor]
> Give me and you shall receive me again'

and it added, in a rather flat Brahminic tongue: 'In this world and in the other what is given is received again.' [57] A very old code states that Anna, food deified, proclaimed the following verse:

> 'Him who, without giving me to the gods or the
>   spirits, or to his servants or guests,
>   prepares and eats [me], and in
>   his folly thus eats poison, I eat him,
>   I am his death.

'But for him who offers the *angihotra*, and then
    eats—in happiness, purity and faith—
    whatever remains after he has fed those
    whom it is his pleasure and duty to feed,
    for him I become ambrosia and he takes pleasure in
      me.' [58]

It is in the nature of food to be shared; to fail to give others a part is to 'kill its essence', to destroy it for oneself and for others. Such is the interpretation at once materialistic and idealistic, that Brahminism gave to charity and hospitality.[59] Wealth is made to be given away. Were there no Brahmins to receive it, 'vain would be the wealth of the rich'. 'He who eats without knowledge kills his food, and his food kills him.' [60] Avarice interrupts the action of food which, when properly treated, is always productive of more.

In this game of exchanges, as well as with reference to theft, Brahminism makes a clear recognition of personal property. The property of the Brahmin is the Brahmin himself. 'The Brahmin's cow is poison, a venomous snake', says the *Veda* of the magicians.[61] The old code of Baudhayana proclaims: 'The property of the Brahmin slays [the guilty] through the son and the grandson; the poison is not [poison]; property of the Brahmin is called [real] poison.' [62] It contains its sanction within itself, since it is in fact that which is terrible about the Brahmin. It is not necessary even that the theft of a Brahmin's property should be conscious and intentional. A section of the *Parvan*,[63] the part of the *Mahabharata* which is most relevant, tells how Nrga, king of the Yadus, was transformed into a lizard for having given, through the fault of his people, a cow to a Brahmin which was another Brahmin's property. The man who received it would not part with it, even for a hundred thousand others; it was a part of his house and belonged to himself: 'She is used to my ways, she is a good milker, placid and attached to me. Her milk is sweet, and I always keep some in my house. She feeds a little child of mine who is weak and already weaned. I cannot give her away.' Nor did the Brahmin from whom she was taken accept another. She was the property of both the Brahmins irrevocably. Caught between the two refusals the unhappy king had remained under a spell these thousands of years through the curse which the refusals entailed.[64]

Nowhere is the connection between the thing given and the donor, or between property and its owner, more clearly apparent than in the rules relating to gifts of cattle.[65] They are well known. King Dharma (Law), Yudhisthira himself, the principal hero of the epic, lived among cattle, ate barley and cowdung and slept on the ground and thus became 'bull' among kings.[66] For three days and nights the owner of cattle to be given away would imitate him and observe the 'cattle oath'. He lived exclusively on 'cattle juices'—water, dung and urine—for one night out of the three. (Urine is the residence of Cri, Fortune.) For one night out of the three he slept with the cattle on the ground and, adds the commentator, 'without scratching himself or removing his vermin', identified himself with them in spirit.[67] When he went to the stall and called them by their sacred names,[68] he added: 'The cow is my mother, the bull is my father' and so on. He repeated the first formula during the act of transfer. After praising the cattle the donor said: 'What you are, I am; today I become of your essence, and giving you I give myself.'[69] And the recipient when he got them (making the *pratighrana*[70]) said: 'Transmitted in spirit, received in spirit, glorify us both, you who have the forms of the sun and moon [Soma and Ugra].'[71]

Other principles of Brahminic law awaken reminiscences of certain Polynesian, Melanesian and American customs we have described. The manner of receiving the gift is curiously similar. The Brahmin has invincible pride. He refuses to have anything to do with markets.[72] In a national economy with towns, markets and money, the Brahmin remains faithful to the economy and morality of the old Indo-Iranian shepherds and other aboriginal peasants of the great plains. He maintains the dignity of a nobleman in taking offence at favours towards him.[73] Two sections of the *Mahabharata* tell how the seven *rsi*,

the great prophets and their disciples, as they went in time of
famine to eat the body of the son of the king Cibi, refused great
gifts and golden figs offered them by the king Caivya Vrsadar-
bha, and answered him: 'O King, to receive from kings is
honey at first but ends as poison.'

This is a quaint theory. A whole caste which lives by gifts
pretends to refuse them,[74] then compromises and accepts only
those which are offered spontaneously.[75] Then it draws up long
lists of persons from whom,[76] and circumstances in which, one
may accept gifts, and of the things [77] which one may accept;
and finally admits everything in the case of a famine [78]—on
condition, to be sure, of some slight purification.[79]

The bond that the gift creates between the donor and the
recipient is too strong for them. As in all systems we have
studied so far, as well as in others, the one is bound too closely
to the other. The recipient is in a state of dependence upon the
donor.[80] It is for this reason that the Brahmin may not accept
and still less solicit from the king. Divinity among divinities,
he is superior to the king and would lose his superiority if
he did other than simply take from him. On the side of the
king his manner of giving is as important as the fact that he
gives.[81]

The gift is thus something that must be given, that must be
received and that is, at the same time, dangerous to accept.
The gift itself constitutes an irrevocable link especially when
it is a gift of food. The recipient depends upon the temper of
the donor,[82] in fact each depends upon the other. Thus a man
does not eat with his enemy.[83]

All kinds of precautions are taken. The authors of the Codes
and Epics spread themselves as only Hindu authors can on the
theme that gifts, donors and things given are to be considered
in their context, precisely and scrupulously, so that there may
be no mistake about the manner of giving and receiving to fit
each particular occasion.[84] There is etiquette at every step. It is
not the same as a market where a man takes a thing objectively
for a price. Nothing is casual here.[85] Contracts, alliances,
transmission of goods, bonds created by these transfers—each

stage in the process is regulated morally and economically. The nature and intention of the contracting parties and the nature of the thing given are indivisible. The lawyer poet expresses perfectly what we want to describe: 'Here is but one wheel turning in one direction.' [86]

3. PLEDGE AND GIFT (GERMANIC SOCIETIES)

If Germanic societies have not preserved for us such old and meaningful traces of their theory of the gift as the Indian, they had none the less a clearly developed system of exchange with gifts voluntarily and obligatorily given, received and repaid. Few systems are so typical. [87]

Germanic civilization, too, was a long time without markets. [88] It remained essentially feudal and peasant; the notion and even the terms of price, purchase and sale seem to be of recent origin. [89] In earlier times it had developed the potlatch and more particularly the system of gift exchange to an extreme degree. Clans within tribes, great extended families within the clans, tribes between themselves, chiefs and even kings, were not confined morally and economically to the closed circles of their own groups; and links, alliances and mutual assistance came into being by means of the pledge, the hostage and the feast or other acts of generosity. [90] We have already seen the litany on gifts taken from the *Havamal*. There are three other facts to note.

An intensive study of the rich German vocabulary derived from the words *geben* and *Gaben* has never been undertaken. [91] They are extraordinarily numerous: *Ausgabe, Abgabe, Hingabe, Liebesgabe, Morgengabe*, the curious *Trostgabe, vergeben, widergeben* and *wiedergeben, Gift* and *Mitgift*, etc. The study, too, of the institutions designated by these words has still to be made. [92] On the other hand, the system of gifts, including the obligation to repay, and its importance in tradition and folklore are admirably described by Richard Meyer in one of the best existing works on folklore. [93] We simply mention it and retain for the moment some remarks on the obligatory force of the bond, the *Angebinde*, constituted by exchange, the offer, the acceptance of the offer and the obligation to repay.

There is another institution of great economic significance which persisted until quite recently and which no doubt is still to be found in some German villages. This is the *Gaben*, the exact equivalent of the Hindu *adanam*.[94] On days of baptism, first communion, betrothal and marriage the guests, comprising often the whole village, give presents whose total value exceeds the cost of the ceremony. In some districts of Germany this *Gaben* constitutes the bride's dowry, given on the wedding morning, and is known as the *Morgengabe*. In places the abundance of these gifts is said to be a measure of the fertility of the young couple.[95] The entry into marital relations and the different gifts which the god-parents hand over at various stages of their career to qualify and help their charges are equally important. This theme is still recognized in French customs, tales and forms of invitation, in the curses of people not invited and the blessings and generosity of those who are.

Another institution has the same origin—the pledge in all kinds of Germanic contracts.[96] The French word *gage* is connected with *wadium* (cf. *wage*). Huvelin shows that the Germanic *wadium* provides a means of understanding the contractual bond and compares it with the Roman *nexum*.[97] In fact, in the manner in which Huvelin interprets it, the pledge accepted allows the contracting parties in Germanic law to react on each other, because one possesses something of the other who, having once owned it, might well have put a spell on it; or else because the pledge is split in two, a half being kept by each partner. But we can suggest a more direct interpretation. The magical sanction may intervene but it is not the sole bond. The thing given as a pledge *must* be given. In Germanic law each contract, sale or purchase, loan or deposit, entails a pledge: one partner is given an object, generally something of little value like a glove or a piece of money (*Treugeld*), a knife, or perhaps—as with the French—a pin or two, and this is returned when the thing handed over is paid for. Huvelin has already noted that the thing is something ordinary, personal or of little value; and he rightly compares this with the theme of the 'life-token'. The pledge thus given is in fact imbued with the personality of the partner who gave it. The fact that it is in the hands of the recipient moves its donor to fulfil his part of the contract and buy himself back by buying the thing. Thus the *nexum* is in the thing used as a pledge and not only in the magical acts or the solemn forms of the contract, the words, oaths ritual and handshakes exchanged; it is present not only in the acts of magical significance, the tallies of which each partner keeps a share, or the joint meals where each partakes of the other's substance; it is present in the thing as well.

Two characteristics of the *wadiatio* prove the presence of this power in the thing. First the pledge not only creates obligations and acts as a binding force but it also engages the honour, authority and *mana* of the man who hands it over.[98] He remains in an inferior position so long as he is not freed from his 'engagement-wager'. For the words *Wette* and *wetten*,[99] translations of *wadium*, imply wager as much as pledge. It is the price of an agreement and the recognition of a challenge, even more than a means of constraining the debtor. As long as the contract is not terminated it is a wager lost, and thus the contractor loses more than he bargained for—not counting the fact that he is liable to lose the thing received which its owner is at liberty to reclaim so long as the pledge is not honoured. The other characteristic shows the danger of receiving the pledge. For it is not only the person who gives it that is bound, but also the one who receives it. As with the recipient in the Trobriands he distrusts the thing given. Thus it is thrown at his feet; if it is a *festuca notata* with runic characters, or a tally of which he is to keep a part, he receives it on the ground or in his breast but never in his hands.[100] The whole ritual takes the form of challenge and distrust, and is an expression of them. In English, 'to throw down the gage' is the equivalent of 'to throw down the gauntlet'. The fact is that the pledge as a thing given spells danger for the two parties concerned.

Here is a third point. The danger represented by the thing given or transmitted is possibly nowhere better expressed than in very ancient Germanic languages. This explains the double meaning of the word *Gift* as gift and poison. Elsewhere we have given a semantic history of this word.[101] The theme of the fateful gift, the present or possession that turns into poison, is fundamental in Germanic folklore. The Rhine Gold is fatal to the man who wins it, the Cup of Hagen is disastrous to the hero who drinks of it; numerous tales and legends of this kind, Germanic and Celtic, still haunt our imaginations. We may quote the stanza in which the hero of the *Edda*, Hreidmar, replies to the curses of Loki:

> 'Thou hast given presents
> But thou hast not given presents of love,
> Thou hast not given of a benevolent heart;
> Thou hadst already been deprived of thy life,
> Had I but known the danger sooner.' [102]

Chinese Law

Finally a great civilization, the Chinese, has preserved from archaic times the very legal principle that interests us: it recognizes the indissoluble bond of a thing with its original owner. Even today the man who sells property, even personal property, retains the right during the rest of his life to 'weep over it'.[103] Father Hoang brought to notice copies of these 'mourning licences' as given by the buyer to the vendor.[104] A kind of 'right of pursuit' is established over the thing combined with a right of pursuit over its owner, and the vendor retains this right long after the thing has fallen into other hands and all the terms of the 'irrevocable' contract have been fulfilled. Because of the thing transmitted (and whether it depreciates or not) the alliance contracted is not temporary, and the contracting parties are bound in perpetual interdependence.

As for Annamite custom Westermarck [105] noted that it was dangerous to receive a gift, and perceived some of the significance of this fact.

CHAPTER IV

CONCLUSIONS

I. MORAL CONCLUSIONS

L ET us extend our observations to the present day. Much of our everyday morality is concerned with the question of obligation and spontaneity in the gift. It is our good fortune that all is not yet couched in terms of purchase and sale. Things have values which are emotional as well as material; indeed in some cases the values are entirely emotional. Our morality is not solely commercial. We still have people and classes who uphold past customs and we bow to them on special occasions and at certain periods of the year.

The gift not yet repaid debases the man who accepted it, particularly if he did so without thought of return. In recalling Emerson's curious essay *On Gifts and Presents* we are not leaving the Germanic field; charity wounds him who receives, and our whole moral effort is directed towards suppressing the unconscious harmful patronage of the rich almoner.[1]

Just as a courtesy has to be returned, so must an invitation. Here we find traces of the traditional basis, the aristocratic potlatch; and we see at work also some of the fundamental motives of human activity: emulation between individuals of the same sex, the basic 'imperialism' of men—of origin part social, part animal or psychological no doubt.[2] In the distinctive sphere of our social life we can never remain at rest. We must always return more than we receive; the return is always bigger and more costly. A family of my childhood in Lorraine, which was forced to a most frugal existence, would face ruin for the sake of its guests on Saints' Days, weddings, first communions and funerals. You had to be a *grand seigneur* on these occasions. Some of our people behave like this all the time and spend money recklessly on their guests, parties and New Year gifts.

Invitations have to be offered and have to be accepted. This usage still exists in our present-day liberal societies. Scarcely fifty years ago, and perhaps more recently in some parts of France and Germany, the whole village would take part in a wedding feast; if anyone held away it was an indication of jealousy and at the same time a fateful omen. In many districts of France everyone still has a part in the proceedings. In Provence on the birth of a child folk still bring along their egg or some other symbolic present.

Things sold have their personality even nowadays. At Cornimont, in a valley in the Vosges, the following custom prevailed a short time ago and may perhaps still be found in some families: in order that animals should forget their former masters and not be tempted to go back to them, a cross was made on the lintel of the stable door, the vendor's halter was retained and the animals were hand-fed with salt. At Raon-aux-Bois a small butter-tart was carried thrice round the dairy and offered to the animals with the right hand. Numerous other French customs show how it is necessary to detach the thing sold from the man who sells it; a thing may be slapped, a sheep may be whipped when sold, and so on.[3]

It appears that the whole field of industrial and commercial law is in conflict with morality. The economic prejudices of the people and producers derive from their strong desire to pursue the thing they have produced once they realize that they have given their labour without sharing in the profits.

Today the ancient principles are making their influence felt upon the rigours, abstractions and inhumanities of our codes. From this point of view much of our law is in process of reformulation and some of our innovations consist in putting back the clock. This reaction against Roman and Saxon insensibility in our régime is a good thing. We can interpret in this way some of the more recent developments in our laws and customs.

It took a long time for artistic, literary or scientific ownership to be recognized beyond the right to sell the manuscript, invention, or work of art. Societies have little interest in admitting that the heirs of an author or inventor—who are, after all, their benefactors—have more than a few paltry rights in the things created. These are readily acclaimed as products of the collective as well as the individual mind, and hence to be public property. However, the scandal of the increment value of paintings, sculptures and *objets d'art* inspired the French law of September 1923 which gives the artist and his heirs and claimants a 'right of pursuit' over the successive increments of his works.

French legislation on social insurance, and accomplished state socialism, are inspired by the principle that the worker gives his life and labour partly to the community and partly to his bosses. If the worker has to collaborate in the business of insurance then those who benefit from his services are not square with him simply by paying him a wage. The State, representing the community, owes him and his management and fellow-workers a certain security in his life against unemployment, sickness, old age and death.

In the same way some ingenious innovations like the family funds freely and enthusiastically provided by industrialists for workers with families, are an answer to the need for employers to get men attached to them and to realize their responsibilities and the degree of material and moral interest that these responsibilities entail. In Great Britain the long period of unemployment affecting millions of workers gave rise to a movement for compulsory unemployment insurance organized by unions. The cities and the State were slow to support the high cost of paying the workless, whose condition arose from that of industry and the market; but some distinguished economists and captains of industry saw that industries themselves should organize unemployment savings and make the necessary sacrifices. They wanted the cost of the workers' security against unemployment to form a part of the expenses of the industry concerned.

We believe that such ideas and legislation correspond not

to an upheaval, but to a return to law.[4] We are seeing the dawn and realization of professional morality and corporate law. The compensation funds and mutual societies which industrial groups are forming in favour of labour have, in the eyes of pure morality, only one flaw: their administration is in the hands of the bosses. But there is also group activity; the State, municipalities, public assistance establishments, works managements and wage-earners are all associated, for instance, in the social legislation of Germany and Alsace-Lorraine, and will shortly be in France. Thus we are returning to a group morality.

On the other hand, it is the individual that the State and the groups within the State want to look after. Society wants to discover the social 'cell'. It seeks the individual in a curious frame of mind in which the sentiments of its own laws are mingled with other, purer sentiments: charity, social service and solidarity. The theme of the gift, of freedom and obligation in the gift, of generosity and self-interest in giving, reappear in our own society like the resurrection of a dominant motif long forgotten.

But a mere statement of what is taking place is not enough. We should deduce from it some course of action or moral precept. It is not sufficient to say that law is in the process of shedding an abstraction—the distinction between real and personal law—or that it is adding some fresh rules to the ill-made legislation on sale and payment for services. We want to show also that the transformation is a good one.

We are returning, as indeed we must do, to the old theme of 'noble expenditure'. It is essential that, as in Anglo-Saxon countries and so many contemporary societies, savage and civilized, the rich should come once more, freely or by obligation, to consider themselves as the treasurers, as it were, of their fellow-citizens. Of the ancient civilizations from which ours has arisen some had the jubilee, others the liturgy, the choragus, the trierarchy, the syssita or the obligatory expenses of the aedile or consular official. We should return to customs of this sort. Then we need better care of the individual's life, health and education, his family and its future. We need more good faith, sympathy and generosity in the contracts of hire and service, rents and sale of the necessities of life. And we have to find the means of limiting the fruits of speculation and usury. Meanwhile the individual must work and be made to rely more upon himself than upon others. From another angle he must defend his group's interest as well as his own. Communism and too much generosity is as harmful to him and society as the selfishness of our contemporaries or the individualism of our laws. In the *Mahabharata* a malignant wood spirit explains to a Brahmin who has given too much away to the wrong people: 'That is why you are thin and pale.' The life of the monk and the life of Shylock are both to be avoided. This new morality will consist of a happy medium between the ideal and the real.

Hence we should return to the old and elemental. Once again we shall discover those motives of action still remembered by many societies and classes: the joy of giving in public, the delight in generous artistic expenditure, the pleasure of hospitality in the public or private feast. Social insurance, solicitude in mutuality or co-operation, in the professional group and all those moral persons called Friendly Societies, are better than the mere personal security guaranteed by the nobleman to his tenant, better than the mean life afforded by the daily wage handed out by managements, and better even than the uncertainty of capitalist savings.

We can visualize a society in which these principles obtain. In the liberal professions of our great nations such a moral and economic system is to some degree in evidence. For honour, disinterestedness and corporate solidarity are not vain words, nor do they deny the necessity for work. We should humanize the other liberal professions and make all of them more perfect. That would be a great deed, and one which Durkheim already had in view.

In doing this we should, we believe, return to the ever-present bases of law, to its real fundamentals and to the very heart of normal social life. There is no need to wish that the citizen should be too subjective, too insensitive or too realistic. He should be vividly aware of himself, of others and of the social reality (and what other reality is there in these moral matters?). He must act with full realization of himself, of society and its sub-groups. The basis of moral action is general; it is common to societies of the highest degree of evolution, to those of the future and to societies of the least advancement. Here we touch bedrock. We are talking no longer in terms of law. We are talking of men and groups since it is they, society, and their sentiments that are in action all the time.

Let us demonstrate this point. What we call total prestation —prestation between clan and clan in which individuals and groups exchange everything between them—constitutes the oldest economic system we know. It is the base from which gift-exchange arose. Now it is precisely this same type towards which we are striving to have our own society—on its own scale —directed. The better to visualize these distant epochs we give two examples from widely differing societies.

In a corroboree of Pine Mountain (East Central Queensland) each person enters the sacred place in turn, his spearthrower in one hand and the other hand behind his back; he lobs his weapon to the far end of the dancing ground, shouting at the same time the name of the place he comes from, like: 'Kunyan is my home'. He stands still for a moment while his friends put gifts, a spear, a boomerang or other weapon, into his other hand. 'Thus a good warrior may get more than his hand can hold, particularly if he has marriageable daughters.' [5]

In the Winnebago tribe clan chiefs make speeches to chiefs of other clans; these are characteristic examples of a ceremonial which is widespread among North American Indian civilizations.[6] At the clan feast each clan cooks food and prepares tobacco for the representatives of other clans. Here by way of illustration are extracts from the speeches given by the Snake Clan chief: 'I salute you; it is well; how could I say otherwise? I am a poor man of no worth and you have remembered me. You have thought of the spirits and you have come to sit with me. And so your dishes will soon be filled, and I salute you again, you men who take the place of the spirits. . . .' When one of the chiefs has eaten, an offering of tobacco is put in the fire and the final sentences express the moral significance of the feast and the prestations: 'I thank you for coming to fill my places and I am grateful to you. You have encouraged me. The blessings of your grandfathers [who had revelations and whom you incarnate] are equal to those of the spirits. It is good that you have partaken of my feast. It must be that our grandfathers have said: "Your life is weak and can be strengthened only by the advice of the warriors." You have helped me and that means life to me.' [7]

A wise precept has run right through human evolution, and we would be as well to adopt it as a principle of action. We should come out of ourselves and regard the duty of giving as a liberty, for in it there lies no risk. A fine Maori proverb runs:

'*Ko maru kai atu*
Ko maru kai mai,
Ka ngohe ngohe.'

'Give as much as you receive and all is for the best.' [8]

2. POLITICAL AND ECONOMIC CONCLUSIONS

Our facts do more than illumine our morality and point out our ideal; for they help us to analyse economic facts of a more general nature, and our analysis might suggest the way to better administrative procedures for our societies.

We have repeatedly pointed out how this economy of gift-exchange fails to conform to the principles of so-called natural economy or utilitarianism. The phenomena in the economic life of the people we have studied (and they are good representatives of the great neolithic stage of civilization) and the survivals of these traditions in societies closer to ours and even in our own custom, are disregarded in the schemes adopted by the few economists who have tried to compare the various forms of economic life. [9] We add our own observations to those of Malinowski who devoted a whole work to ousting the prevalent doctrines on primitive economics. [10]

Here is a chain of undoubted fact. The notion of value exists in these societies. Very great surpluses, even by European

standards, are amassed; they are expended often at pure loss
with tremendous extravagance and without a trace of mer-
cenariness; [11] among things exchanged are tokens of wealth, a
kind of money. All this very rich economy is nevertheless
imbued with religious elements; money still has its magical
power and is linked to clan and individual. Diverse economic
activities—for example, the market—are impregnated with
ritual and myth; they retain a ceremonial character, obligatory
and efficacious; [12] they have their own ritual and etiquette.
Here is the answer to the question already posed by Durkheim
about the religious origin of the notion of economic value.[13]
The facts also supply answers to a string of problems about the
forms and origins of what is so badly termed exchange—the
barter or *permutatio* of useful articles.[14] In the view of cautious
Latin authors in the Aristotelian tradition and their *a priori*
economic history, this is the origin of the division of labour.[15]
On the contrary, it is something other than utility which makes
goods circulate in these multifarious and fairly enlightened
societies. Clans, age groups and sexes, in view of the many
relationships ensuing from contacts between them, are in a
state of perpetual economic effervescence which has little about
it that is materialistic; it is much less prosaic than our sale and
purchase, hire of services and speculations.

We may go farther than this and break down, reconsider
and redefine the principal notions of which we have already
made use. Our terms 'present' and 'gift' do not have precise
meanings, but we could find no others. Concepts which we like
to put in opposition—freedom and obligation; generosity,
liberality, luxury on the one hand and saving, interest, austerity
on the other—are not exact and it would be well to put them
to the test. We cannot deal very fully with this; but let us take
an example from the Trobriands. It is a complex notion that
inspires the economic actions we have described, a notion
neither of purely free and gratuitous prestations, nor of purely
interested and utilitarian production and exchange; it is a
kind of hybrid.

Malinowski made a serious effort to classify all the transactions he witnessed in the Trobriands according to the interest or disinterestedness present in them. He ranges them from pure gift to barter with bargaining, but this classification is untenable.[16] Thus according to Malinowski the typical 'pure gift' is that between spouses. Now in our view one of the most important acts noted by the author, and one which throws a strong light on sexual relationships, is the *mapula*, the sequence of payments by a husband to his wife as a kind of salary for sexual services.[17] Likewise the payments to chiefs are tribute; the distributions of food (*sagali*) are payments for labour or ritual accomplished, such as work done on the eve of a funeral.[18] Thus basically as these gifts are not spontaneous so also they are not really disinterested. They are for the most part counter-prestations made not solely in order to pay for goods or services, but also to maintain a profitable alliance which it would be unwise to reject, as for instance partnership between fishing tribes and tribes of hunters and potters.[19] Now this fact is widespread—we have met it with the Maori, Tsimshian and others.[20] Thus it is clear wherein this mystical and practical force resides, which at once binds clans together and keeps them separate, which divides their labour and constrains them to exchange. Even in these societies the individuals and the groups, or rather the sub-groups, have always felt the sovereign right to refuse a contract, and it is this which lends an appearance of generosity to the circulation of goods. On the other hand, normally they had neither the right of, nor interest in, such a refusal; and it is that which makes these distant societies seem akin to ours.

The use of money suggests other considerations. The Trobriand *vaygu'a*, armshells and necklaces, like the North-West American coppers and Iroquois *wampum*, are at once wealth, tokens of wealth,[21] means of exchange and payment, and things to be given away or destroyed. In addition they are pledges, linked to the persons who use them and who in turn are bound by them. Since, however, at other times they serve as tokens of money, there is interest in giving them away, for if they are transformed into services or merchandise that yield money then

one is better off in the end. We may truly say that the Trobriand or Tsimshian chief behaves somewhat like the capitalist
who knows how to spend his money at the right time only to
build his capital up again. Interest and disinterestedness taken
together explain this form of the circulation of wealth and of
the circulation of tokens of wealth that follows upon it.

Even the destruction of wealth does not correspond to the
complete disinterestedness which one might expect. These
great acts of generosity are not free from self-interest. The
extravagant consumption of wealth, particularly in the potlatch, always exaggerated and often purely destructive, in
which goods long stored are all at once given away or destroyed,
lends to these institutions the appearance of wasteful expenditure and child-like prodigality.[22] Not only are valuable goods
thrown away and foodstuffs consumed to excess but there is
destruction for its own sake—coppers are thrown into the sea
or broken. But the motives of such excessive gifts and reckless
consumption, such mad losses and destruction of wealth,
especially in these potlatch societies, are in no way disinterested.
Between vassals and chiefs, between vassals and their henchmen,
the hierarchy is established by means of these gifts. To give is
to show one's superiority, to show that one is something more
and higher, that one is *magister*. To accept without returning or
repaying more is to face subordination, to become a client and
subservient, to become *minister*.

The magic ritual in the *kula* known as *mwasila* contains
spells and symbols which show that the man who wants to enter
into a contract seeks above all profit in the form of social—
one might almost say animal—superiority. Thus he charms the
betel-nut to be used with his partners, casts a spell over the
chief and his fellows, then over his own pigs, his necklaces, his
head and mouth, the opening gifts and whatever else he carries;
then he chants, not without exaggeration: 'I shall kick the
mountain, the mountain moves . . . the mountain falls down.
. . . My spell shall go to the top of Dobu Mountain. . . . My
canoe will sink. . . . My fame is like thunder, my treading is
like the roar of flying witches. . . . Tudududu.'[23] The aim is to

be the first, the finest, luckiest, strongest and richest and that is how to set about it. Later the chief confirms his *mana* when he redistributes to his vassals and relatives what he has just received; he maintains his rank among the chiefs by exchanging armshells for necklaces, hospitality for visits, and so on. In this case wealth is, in every aspect, as much a thing of prestige as a thing of utility. But are we certain that our own position is different and that wealth with us is not first and foremost a means of controlling others?

Let us test now the notion to which we have opposed the ideas of the gift and disinterestedness: that of interest and the individual pursuit of utility. This agrees no better with previous theories. If similar motives animate Trobriand and American chiefs and Andaman clans and once animated generous Hindu or Germanic noblemen in their giving and spending, they are not to be found in the cold reasoning of the business man, banker or capitalist. In those earlier civilizations one had interests but they differed from those of our time. There, if one hoards, it is only to spend later on, to put people under obligations and to win followers. Exchanges are made as well, but only of luxury objects like clothing and ornaments, or feasts and other things that are consumed at once. Return is made with interest, but that is done in order to humiliate the original donor or exchange partner and not merely to recompense him for the loss that the lapse of time causes him. He has an interest but it is only analogous to the one which we say is our guiding principle.

Ranged between the relatively amorphous and disinterested economy within the sub-groups of Australian and North American (Eastern and Prairie) clans, and the individualistic economy of pure interest which our societies have had to some extent ever since their discovery by Greeks and Semites, there is a great series of institutions and economic events not governed by the rationalism which past theory so readily took for granted.

The word 'interest' is recent in origin and can be traced back to the Latin *interest* written on account books opposite

rents to be recovered. In the most epicurean of these philoso-
phies pleasure and the good were pursued and not material
utility. The victory of rationalism and mercantilism was
required before the notions of profit and the individual were
given currency and raised to the level of principles. One can
date roughly—after Mandeville and his *Fable des Abeilles*—the
triumph of the notion of individual interest. It is only by
awkward paraphrasing that one can render the phrase 'individual interest' in Latin, Greek or Arabic. Even the men who
wrote in classical Sanskrit and used the word *artha*, which is
fairly close to our idea of interest, turned it, as they did with
other categories of action, into an idea different from ours. The
sacred books of ancient India divide human actions into the
categories of law (*dharma*), interest (*artha*) and desire (*kama*).
But *artha* refers particularly to the political interest of king,
Brahmins and ministers, or royalty and the various castes.
The considerable literature of the *Niticastra* is not economic
in tone.

It is only our Western societies that quite recently turned
man into an economic animal. But we are not yet all animals
of the same species. In both lower and upper classes pure
irrational expenditure is in current practice: it is still characteristic of some French noble houses. *Homo oeconomicus* is not
behind us, but before, like the moral man, the man of duty, the
scientific man and the reasonable man. For a long time man
was something quite different; and it is not so long now since
he became a machine—a calculating machine.

In other respects we are still far from frigid utilitarian
calculation. Make a thorough statistical analysis, as Halbwachs did for the working classes, of the consumption and
expenditure of our middle classes and how many needs are
found satisfied? How many desires are fulfilled that have
utility as their end? Does not the rich man's expenditure on
luxury, art, servants and extravagances recall the expenditure
of the nobleman of former times or the savage chiefs whose
customs we have been describing?

It is another question to ask if it is good that this should be so. It is a good thing possibly that there exist means of expenditure and exchange other than economic ones. However, we contend that the best economic procedure is not to be found in the calculation of individual needs. I believe that we must become, in proportion as we would develop our wealth, something more than better financiers, accountants and administrators. The mere pursuit of individual ends is harmful to the ends and peace of the whole, to the rhythm of its work and pleasures, and hence in the end to the individual.

We have just seen how important sections and groups of our capital industries are seeking to attach groups of their employees to them. Again all the syndicalist groups, employers' as much as wage-earners', claim that they are defending and representing the general interest with a fervour equal to that of the particular interests of their members, or of the interests of the groups themselves. Their speeches are burnished with many fine metaphors. Nevertheless, one has to admit that not only ethics and philosophy, but also economic opinion and practice, are starting to rise to this 'social' level. The feeling is that there is no better way of making men work than by reassuring them of being paid loyally all their lives for labour which they give loyally not only for their own sakes but for that of others. The producer-exchanger feels now as he has always felt—but this time he feels it more acutely—that he is giving something of himself, his time and his life. Thus he wants recompense, however modest, for this gift. And to refuse him this recompense is to incite him to laziness and lower production.

We draw now a conclusion both sociological and practical. The famous Sura LXIV, 'Mutual Deception', given at Mecca to Mohammed, says:

15. Your possessions and your children are only a trial and Allah it is with whom is a great reward.

16. Therefore be careful [of your duty to] Allah as much as you can, and hear and obey and spend (*sadaqa*), it is better for your souls; and whoever is saved from the greediness of his soul, these it is that are the successful.

17. If you set apart from Allah a goodly portion, He will double it for you and forgive you; and Allah is the multiplier of rewards, forbearing.

18. The knower of the unseen and the seen, the mighty, the wise.

Replace the name of Allah by that of the society or professional group, or unite all three; replace the concept of alms by that of co-operation, of a prestation altruistically made; you will have a fair idea of the practice which is now coming into being. It can be seen at work already in certain economic groups and in the hearts of the masses who often enough know their own interest and the common interest better than their leaders do.

3. Sociological and Ethical Conclusions

We may be permitted another note about the method we have used. We do not set this work up as a model; it simply proffers one or two suggestions. It is incomplete: the analysis could be pushed farther.[24] We are really posing questions for historians and anthropologists and offering possible lines of research for them rather than resolving a problem and laying down definite answers. It is enough for us to be sure for the moment that we have given sufficient data for such an end.

This being the case, we would point out that there is a heuristic element in our manner of treatment. The facts we have studied are all 'total' social phenomena. The word 'general' may be preferred although we like it less. Some of the facts presented concern the whole of society and its institutions (as with potlatch, opposing clans, tribes on visit, etc.); others, in which exchanges and contracts are the concern of individuals, embrace a large number of institutions.

These phenomena are at once legal, economic, religious, aesthetic, morphological and so on. They are legal in that they concern individual and collective rights, organized and diffuse morality; they may be entirely obligatory, or subject simply to praise or disapproval. They are at once political and domestic, being of interest both to classes and to clans and families. They are religious; they concern true religion, animism, magic and diffuse religious mentality. They are economic, for the notions of value, utility, interest, luxury, wealth, acquisition, accumulation, consumption and liberal and sumptuous expenditure are all present, although not perhaps in their modern senses. Moreover, these institutions have an important aesthetic side which we have left unstudied; but the dances performed, the songs and shows, the dramatic representations given between camps or partners, the objects made, used, decorated, polished, amassed and transmitted with affection, received with joy, given away in triumph, the feasts in which everyone participates—all these, the food, objects and services, are the source of aesthetic emotions as well as emotions aroused by interest.[25] This is true not only of Melanesia but also, and particularly, of the potlatch of North-West America and still more true of the market-festival of the Indo-European world. Lastly, our phenomena are clearly morphological. Everything that happens in the course of gatherings, fairs and markets or in the feasts that replace them, presupposes groups whose duration exceeds the season of social concentration, like the winter potlatch of the Kwakiutl or the few weeks of the Melanesian maritime expeditions. Moreover, in order that these meetings may be carried out in peace, there must be roads or water for transport and tribal, inter-tribal or international alliances—*commercium* and *connubium*.[26]

We are dealing then with something more than a set of themes, more than institutional elements, more than institutions, more even than systems of institutions divisible into legal, economic, religious and other parts. We are concerned with 'wholes', with systems in their entirety. We have not described them as if they were fixed, in a static or skeletal condition, and still less have we dissected them into the rules and myths and values and so on of which they are composed. It is only by considering them as wholes that we have been able to see their essence, their operation and their living aspect, and to catch the fleeting moment when the society and its members take emotional stock of themselves and their situation as regards others. Only by making such concrete observation of social life is it possible to come upon facts such as those which our study is beginning to reveal. Nothing in our opinion is more urgent or promising than research into 'total' social phenomena.

The advantage is twofold. Firstly there is an advantage in generality, for facts of widespread occurrence are more likely to be universal than local institutions or themes, which are invariably tinged with local colour. But particularly the advantage is in realism. We see social facts in the round, as they really are. In society there are not merely ideas and rules, but also men and groups and their behaviours. We see them in motion as an engineer sees masses and systems, or as we observe octopuses and anemones in the sea. We see groups of men, and active forces, submerged in their environments and sentiments.

Historians believe and justly resent the fact that sociologists make too many abstractions and separate unduly the various elements of society. We should follow their precepts and observe what is given. The tangible fact is Rome or Athens or the average Frenchman or the Melanesian of some island, and not prayer or law as such. Whereas formerly sociologists were obliged to analyse and abstract rather too much, they should now force themselves to reconstitute the whole. This is the way to reach incontestable facts. They will also find a way of satisfying psychologists who have a pronounced viewpoint, and particularly psycho-pathologists, since there is no doubt that the object of their study is concrete. They all observe, or at least ought to, minds as wholes and not minds divided into faculties. We should follow suit. The study of the concrete, which is the study of the whole, is made more readily, is more interesting and furnishes more explanations in the sphere of sociology than the study of the abstract. For we observe complete and complex beings. We too describe them in their organisms and *psychai* as well as in their behaviour as groups, with the attendant psychoses: sentiments, ideas and desires of the crowd, of organized societies and their sub-groups. We see bodies and their reactions, and their ideas and sentiments as interpretations or as motive forces. The aim and principle of sociology is to observe and understand the whole group in its total behaviour.

It is not possible here—it would have meant extending a restricted study unduly—to seek the morphological implications of our facts. It may be worth while, however, to indicate the method one might follow in such a piece of research.

All the societies we have described above with the exception of our European societies are segmentary. Even the Indo-Europeans, the Romans before the Twelve Tables, the Germanic societies up to the *Edda*, and Irish society to the time of its chief literature, were still societies based on the clan or on great families more or less undivided internally and isolated from each other externally. All these were far removed from the degree of unification with which historians have credited them or which is ours today. Within these groups the individuals, even the most influential, were less serious, avaricious and selfish than we are; externally at least they were and are generous and more ready to give. In tribal feasts, in ceremonies of rival clans, allied families or those that assist at each other's initiation, groups visit each other; and with the development of the law of hospitality in more advanced societies, the rules of friendship and the contract are present—along with the gods—to ensure the peace of markets and villages; at these times men meet in a curious frame of mind with exaggerated fear and an equally exaggerated generosity which appear stupid in no one's eyes but our own. In these primitive and archaic societies there is no middle path. There is either complete trust or mistrust. One lays down one's arms, renounces magic and gives everything away, from casual hospitality to one's daughter or one's property. It is in such conditions that men, despite themselves, learnt to renounce what was theirs and made contracts to give and repay.

But then they had no choice in the matter. When two groups of men meet they may move away or in case of mistrust or defiance they may resort to arms; or else they can come to terms. Business has always been done with foreigners, although these might have been allies. The people of Kiriwina said to

Malinowski: 'The Dobu man is not good as we are. He is fierce, he is a man-eater. When we come to Dobu, we fear him, he might kill us! But see! I spit the charmed ginger root and their mind turns. They lay down their spears, they receive us well.'[27] Nothing better expresses how close together lie festival and warfare.

Thurnwald describes with reference to another Melanesian tribe, with genealogical material, an actual event which shows just as clearly how these people pass in a group quite suddenly from a feast to a battle.[28] Buleau, a chief, had invited Bobal, another chief, and his people to a feast which was probably to be the first of a long series. Dances were performed all night long. By morning everyone was excited by the sleepless night of song and dance. On a remark made by Buleau one of Bobal's men killed him; and the troop of men massacred and pillaged and ran off with the women of the village. 'Buleau and Bobal were more friends than rivals' they said to Thurnwald. We all have experience of events like this.

It is by opposing reason to emotion and setting up the will for peace against rash follies of this kind that peoples succeed in substituting alliance, gift and commerce for war, isolation and stagnation.

The research proposed would have some conclusion of this kind. Societies have progressed in the measure in which they, their sub-groups and their members, have been able to stabilize their contracts and to give, receive and repay. In order to trade, man must first lay down his spear. When that is done he can succeed in exchanging goods and persons not only between clan and clan but between tribe and tribe and nation and nation, and above all between individuals. It is only then that people can create, can satisfy their interests mutually and define them without recourse to arms. It is in this way that the clan, the tribe and nation have learnt—just as in the future the classes and nations and individuals will learn—how to oppose one another without slaughter and to give without sacrificing themselves to others. That is one of the secrets of their wisdom and solidarity.

There is no other course feasible. The *Chronicles of Arthur* [29] relate how King Arthur, with the help of a Cornish carpenter, invented the marvel of his court, the miraculous Round Table at which his knights would never come to blows. Formerly because of jealousy, skirmishes, duels and murders had set blood flowing in the most sumptuous of feasts. The carpenter says to Arthur: 'I will make thee a fine table, where sixteen hundred may sit at once, and from which none need be excluded. . . . And no knight will be able to raise combat, for there the highly placed will be on the same level as the lowly.' There was no 'head of the table' and hence no more quarrels. Wherever Arthur took his table, contented and invincible remained his noble company. And this today is the way of the nations that are strong, rich, good and happy. Peoples, classes, families and individuals may become rich, but they will not achieve happiness until they can sit down like the knights around their common riches. There is no need to seek far for goodness and happiness. It is to be found in the imposed peace, in the rhythm of communal and private labour, in wealth amassed and redistributed, in the mutual respect and reciprocal generosity that education can impart.

Thus we see how it is possible under certain circumstances to study total human behaviour; and how that concrete study leads not only to a science of manners, a partial social science, but even to ethical conclusions—'civility', or 'civics' as we say today. Through studies of this sort we can find, measure and assess the various determinants, aesthetic, moral, religious and economic, and the material and demographic factors, whose sum is the basis of society and constitutes the common life, and whose conscious direction is the supreme art—politics in the Socratic sense of the word.

BIBLIOGRAPHICAL ABBREVIATIONS

USED IN THE NOTES

5th, 7th, 9th or *12th Report:* Boas, 'Reports on the Tribes of N.W. Canada' in *British Association for the Advancement of Science*, 1891–8.

11th Census: 'Report on the Population, etc., of Alaska' in *Eleventh Alaskan Census*, 1900.

19 Years: Turner, *Nineteen Years in Polynesia.*

A.M.N.H.: *Report of the American Museum of Natural History.*

Andamans: A. R. Brown (A. R. Radcliffe-Brown), *The Andaman Islanders.*

Anuc.: *Anucasanaparvan*, Book XIII of the *Mahabharata.*

A.R.B.A.E.: *Annual Report of the Bureau of American Ethnology.*

Argonauts: Malinowski, *Argonauts of the Western Pacific.*

A.S.: *L'Année Sociologique.*

B.A.E.: The Bureau of American Ethnology.

Chukchee: Bogoras, 'The Chukchee' in *Jesup North Pacific Expedition*, VII.

Eth. Kwa.: Boas, 'Ethnology of the Kwakiutl', in *Annual Report of the Bureau of American Ethnology*, XXXV.

Foi Jurée: Davy, 'Foi Jurée' in *Travaux de l'Année Sociologique*, 1922.

Forschungen: Thurnwald, *Forschungen auf den Salomo Inseln.*

Haida: Swanton, 'The Haida' in *Jesup North Pacific Expedition*, V.

Haida Texts: Swanton, 'Haida Texts' in *do.*, VI and X.

Haida T. and M.: Swanton, 'Haida Texts and Myths' in *Bulletin of the Bureau of American Ethnology*, no. 29.

H.M.S.: Rivers, *History of the Melanesian Society.*

J.N.P.E.: *Jesup North Pacific Expedition.*

J.P.S.: *Journal of the Polynesian Society.*

J.R.A.I.: *Journal of the Royal Anthropological Institute.*

Koopen: Kruyt, 'Koopen in Midden Celebes' in *Meded. der Konink. Akademie v. Wet., Afd. Letterk.*, 56, series B.

Koryak: Jochelson, 'The Koryak' in *Jesup North Pacific Expedition*, VI.

Kwakiutl: Boas, 'The Kwakiutl Indians' in *do.*, V.

Kwa. T. I: Boas, 'Kwakiutl Texts', First Series, in *do.*, III.

Kwa. T. II: Boas, 'Kwakiutl Texts', Second Series, in *do.*, X.

Magie et Droit: Huvelin, 'Magie et Droit Individuels' in *Année Sociologique*, X.

Manuel: Giraud, *Manuel Elémentaire de Droit Romain*, 7th edn.

M.C.D.: Tregear, *Maori Comparative Dictionary.*

Melanesians: Seligman, *The Melanesians of British New Guinea.*

Prim. Ec.: Malinowski, 'Primitive Economics' in *Economic Journal*, March 1921.

Sec. Soc.: Boas, 'Secret Societies and Social Organization of the Kwakiutl Indians' in *Report of the American Museum of Natural History*, 1895.

Textes: Giraud, *Textes de Droit Romain.*

Tlingit: Swanton, 'The Tlingit Indians' in *Annual Report of the Bureau of American Ethnology*, XXVI.

Tlingit T. and M.: Swanton, 'Tlingit Texts and Myths' in *Bulletin of the Bureau of American Ethnology*, no. 39.

T.N.Z.I.: *Transactions of the New Zealand Institute*.

Tsim. Myth.: Boas, 'Tsimshian Mythology' in *Annual Report of the Bureau of American Ethnology*, XXXI.

Walde: Walde, *Lateinisches Etymologisches Wörterbuch*.

Introductory

[1] Cassel in his *Theory of Social Economy*, Vol. II, p. 345, mentions this text.

[2] I have been unable to consult Burckhard, *Zum Begriff der Schenkung*, pp. 53 ff. But for Anglo-Saxon law our immediate point has been noted by Pollock and Maitland, *History of English Law*, Vol. II, p. 82: 'The wide word "gift" . . . will cover sale, exchange, gage and lease.' Cf. pp. 12, 212–14: 'Perhaps we may doubt whether . . . a purely gratuitous promise . . . would have been enforced.' See also the essay by Neubecker on the Germanic dowry, *Die Mitgift*, 1909, pp. 65 ff.

[3] 'Foi Jurée'; see bibliography in Mauss, 'Une Forme archaique de Contrat chez les Thraces' in *Revue des Etudes Grecques*, 1921; R. Lenoir, 'L'Institution du Potlatch' in *Revue Philosophique*, 1924.

[4] M. F. Samlo, *Der Güterverkehr in der Urgesellschaft*, Institut Solvay, 1909, has some sound discussion on this, and on p. 156 suggests that he is on the lines of our own argument.

[5] Grierson, *Silent Trade*, 1903, argued conclusively against this view. See also Von Moszkowski, *Wirtschaftsleben der primitiven Völker*, 1911; although he considers theft to be primitive and confuses it with the right to take. A good exposition of Maori data is to be found in W. von Brun, 'Wirtschaftsorganisation der Maori' in *Beiträgungen Lamprecht*, 18, 1912, in which a chapter is devoted to exchange. The most recent comprehensive work on so-called primitive economics is Koppers, 'Ethnologische Wirtschaftsordnung', in *Anthropos*, 1915–16, pp. 611–51 and 971–1079; strong on presentation of material but for the rest rather hair-splitting.

[6] We wrote recently that in Australia, especially on a death, there is the beginning of exchange on a tribal basis, and not merely amongst clans and phratries. Among the Kakadu of the Northern Territory there are three mortuary ceremonies. During the third the men have a kind of inquest to find out who is the sorcerer responsible for the death. Contrary to normal Australian custom no feud follows. The men simply gather with their spears and state what they require in exchange. Next day the spears are taken to another tribe, e.g. the Umoriu, who realize the reason for the visit. The spears are piled and in accordance with a known scale the required objects are set before them. Then the Kakadu take them away (Baldwin Spencer, *Tribes of the Northern Territories*, 1914, p. 247). Spencer then states that the objects can then be exchanged for spears, a fact we do not fully understand. But he fails to see the connection between the mortuary ceremony and the exchange of gifts, adding that the natives themselves do not see it. But the custom is easy enough to understand. It is a pact which takes the place of a feud, and which sets up an inter-tribal market. The exchange of objects

is simultaneously an exchange of peace pledges and of sentiments of solidarity in mourning. In Australia this is normally seen only between clans and families which are in some way associated or related by marriage. The only difference here is that the custom is extended to the tribal basis.

[7] A poet as late as Pindar could say νεανίᾳ γαμβρῷ προπίνων οἴκοθεν οἴκαδε, *Olympiads*, VIII, 4. The whole passage still reflects the kind of situation we are describing. The themes of the gift, of wealth, marriage, honour, favour, alliance, of shared food and drink, and the theme of jealousy in marriage are all clearly represented.

[8] See specially the remarkable rules of the ball game among the Omaha: Fletcher and la Flesche, 'Omaha Tribe' in *A.R.B.A.E.*, 1905–6, pp. 197 and 366.

[9] Krause, *Tlingit Indianer*, pp. 234 ff., notes the character of the festivals and rituals although he did not call them 'potlatch'. Boursin in *Eleventh Census*, pp. 54–66, and Porter, ibid. p. 33, saw and named the reciprocal glorification in the potlatch. Swanton, however, has the best commentary, in 'Social Conditions . . . of the Tlingit Indians' in *A.R.B.A.E.*, XXVI, 345. Cf. our notes in *A.S.*, XI, 207 and in *Foi Jurée*, p. 172.

[10] On the meaning of the word potlatch, see Barbeau, *Bulletin de la Société de Géographie de Québec*, 1911, and *Foi Jurée*, p. 162. It seems to us, however, that Davy does not take into account the original meaning of the word. Boas, admittedly for the Kwakiutl and not the Chinook, uses the word 'feeder', although the literal meaning is 'Place of getting Satiated' —*Kwa. T.*, II, p. 43; cf. *Kwa. T.*, I, pp. 255, 517. But the two meanings suggested, gift and food, are not exclusive since the usual content of the gift, here at any rate, is food.

[11] The legal aspect of potlatch has been discussed by Adam in his articles in the *Zeitschrift für vergleichende Rechtswissenschaft* starting 1911, and in the *Festschrift* to Seler, 1920, and by Davy in *Foi Jurée*. The economic and ritual aspects are no less important and merit the same detailed study. The religious nature of the people involved and of the objects exchanged or destroyed have a bearing on the nature of the contracts, as have the values attributed to them.

[12] The Haida call it 'killing wealth'.

[13] See Hunt's documents in *Eth. Kwa.*, p. 1340, where there is an interesting description of the way the clan brings its potlatch contributions to the chief, and a record of some of the discourses. The chief says: 'It will not be in my name. It will be in your name, and you will become famous among the tribes, when it is said that you have given your property for a potlatch' (p. 1342).

[14] The potlatch is not confined to the tribes of the North-West. We consider also the 'Asking Festival' of the Alaskan Eskimo as something more than a mere borrowing from neighbouring Indian tribes.

[15] See our observations in *A.S.*, XI, 101 and XIII, 372–4, and *Anthropologie*, 1920. Lenoir notes two clear potlatch traits in South America, 'Expéditions Maritimes en Mélanésie' in *Anthropologie*, Sept. 1924.

[16] Thurnwald, in *Forschungen*, Vol. III, 1912, p. 8, uses this word.

[17] *Revue des Etudes Grecques*, XXXIV, 1921.

Chapter I

¹ Davy, in *Foi Jurée*, p. 140, studies these exchanges with reference to the marriage contract. Here we point out further implications.

² 19 *Years*, p. 178; *Samoa*, pp. 82 ff.; Stair, *Old Samoa*, p. 75.

³ Krämer, *Samoa-Inseln*, Vol. II, pp. 52–63.

⁴ Stair, *Old Samoa*, p. 180; Turner, 19 *Years*, p. 225; *Samoa*, p. 91.

⁵ Turner, 19 *Years*, p. 184; *Samoa*, p. 91.

⁶ Krämer, *Samoa-Inseln*, Vol. II, p. 105; Turner, *Samoa*, p. 146.

⁷ Krämer, ibid., pp. 96, 313. The *malaga* trading expedition (cf. the *walaga* of New Guinea) is very like the potlatch and characteristic of the neighbouring Melanesian archipelago. Krämer uses the word *Gegenschenk* for the exchange of *oloa* and *tonga* which we shall discuss. We do not intend to follow the exaggerations of the English school of Rivers and Elliot Smith or those of the Americans who, after Boas, see the whole American potlatch as a series of borrowings, but still we grant that an important part is played by the spreading of institutions. It is specially important in this area where trading expeditions go great distances between islands and have done from early times; there must have been transmitted not only the articles of merchandise but also methods of exchange. Malinowski, whom we quote later, recognizes this. See Lenoir, 'Expéditions maritimes en Mélanésie' in *Anthropologie*, 1924.

⁸ Rivalry among Maori clans is often mentioned, particularly with regard to festivals, e.g. by S. P. Smith, *J.P.S.* XV, 87.

⁹ This is not properly potlatch because the counter-prestation lacks the element of usury. But as we shall see with the Maori the fact that no return is made implies the loss of *mana*, or of 'face' as the Chinese say; the same is true for Samoa.

¹⁰ Turner, 19 *Years*, p. 178; *Samoa*, p. 52. The theme of honour through ruin is fundamental to North-West American potlatch.

¹¹ Turner, 19 *Years*, p. 178; *Samoa*, p. 83, says the young man is 'adopted'. This is wrong; it is fosterage. Education is outside his own family certainly, but in fact it marks a return to his uterine family (the father's sister is the spouse of the mother's brother). In Polynesia both maternal and paternal relatives are classificatory. See our review of E. Best, *Maori Nomenclature* in *A.S.*, VII, 420 and Durkheim's remarks in V, 37.

¹² 19 *Years*, p. 179; *Samoa*, p. 83.

¹³ See our remarks on the Fiji *vasu* in 'Procès verbal de l'I.F.A.', *Anthropologie*, 1921.

¹⁴ Krämer, *Samoa-Inseln*, Vol. I, p. 482; Vol. II, p. 90.

¹⁵ Ibid., Vol. II, p. 296. Cf. p. 90 (*toga* equals *Mitgift*); p. 94 exchanges of *oloa* and *toga*.

¹⁶ Ibid., Vol. I, p. 477. Violette, *Dictionnaire Samoan-Français*, defines *toga* as 'native valuables consisting of fine mats, and *oloa* valuables such as houses, cloth, boats, guns'; and he refers back to *oa*, valuables in general.

¹⁷ 19 *Years*, p. 179; cf. p. 186; *M.C.D.*, p. 468 under *taonga* confuses this with *oloa*.

The Rev. Ella, 'Polynesian Native Clothing', in *J.P.S.*, VIII, 165, describes the *ie tonga* (mats); they were 'the chief wealth of the natives; indeed at one time were used as a medium of currency in payment for work, etc., also for barter, interchange of property, at marriage and other special occasions of courtesy. They are often retained in families as heirlooms, and many old *ie* are well known and more highly valued as having belonged to some celebrated family.' Cf. Turner, *Samoa*, p. 120. We shall see that these expressions have their equivalents in Melanesia, in North America and in our own folklore.

[18] Krämer, *Samoa-Inseln*, Vol. II, pp. 90, 93.

[19] See *M.C.D.* under *taonga:* (Tahitian) *tataoa*, to give property, *faataoa*, to compensate; (Marquesan) Lesson, *Polynésiens*, Vol. II, p. 232, *taetae; tiau tae-tae*, presents given, 'local produce given in exchange for foreign goods'. Radiguet, *Derniers Sauvages*, p. 157. The root of the word is *tahu*, etc.

[20] See Mauss, 'Origines de la Notion de la Monnaie' in *Anthropologie*, 1914, where most of the facts quoted, except for Negrito and American material, belong to this domain.

[21] *Proverbs*, p. 103.

[22] *Maori Momentoes*, p. 21.

[23] In *Transactions of the New Zealand Institute*, I, 354.

[24] New Zealand tribes are divided in theory by the Maori themselves into fishermen, agriculturalists and hunters, who are supposed to exchange their produce. Cf. Best, 'Forest-Lore', in *T.N.Z.I.*, XLII, 435.

[25] Ibid., p. 431; translation, p. 439.

[26] The word *hau*, like the Latin *spiritus*, means both wind and soul. More precisely *hau* is the spirit and power of inanimate and vegetable things. The word *mana* is reserved for men and spirits and is not applied to things as much as in Melanesian languages.

[27] *Utu* means satisfaction in blood vengeance.

[28] *He hau*. These sentences were all abridged by Best.

[29] Many facts illustrating this point were collected by R. Hertz in his *Péché et l'Expiation*. They show that the sanction against theft is the mystical effect of the *mana* of the object stolen; moreover, the object is surrounded by taboos and marked by its owner, and has *hau*, spiritual power, as a result. This *hau* avenges theft, controls the thief, bewitches him and leads him to death or constrains him to restore the object.

[30] In Hertz will be found material on the *mauri* to which we allude here. *Mauri* are talismans, safeguards and sanctuaries where the clan soul (*hapu*) dwells with its *mana* and the *hau* of its land.

Best's documents require more comment than we can give here, especially those concerned with *hau whitia* and *kai hau*. See especially 'Spiritual Concepts' in *J.P.S.*, X, 10 (Maori text), and IX, 198. Best translates *hau whitia* well as 'averted *hau*'. The sins of theft, of non-repayment, of non-counter-prestation are a 'turning aside' of the spirit (*hau*) as in the case of a refusal to make an exchange or give a present. *Kai hau* is badly translated as the equivalent of *hau whitia*. It implies the act of eating the soul, and may well be synonymous with *whangai hau* (cf. Tregear,

M.C.D., under *kai* and *whangai*). But *kai* refers to food and the word alludes to the sharing of food and the fault of remaining in debt over it. Further, the word *hau* itself also belongs to the realm of ideas. Williams, *Maori Dictionary*, p. 47, says '*hau*, return present by way of acknowledgement for a present received'.

[31] We draw attention to the expression *kai-hau-kai*, *M.C.D.*, p. 116: 'The return present of food, etc., made by one tribe to another. A feast (in the South).' This signifies that the return gift is really the 'spirit' of the original prestation returning to its point of departure: 'food that is the *hau* of other food.' European vocabularies have not the ability to describe the complexity of these ideas.

[32] The *taonga* seem to have an individuality beyond that of the *hau*, which derives from their relationship with their owner. They bear names. According to the best authorities (*M.C.D.* under *pounamu*, from the manuscript of Colenso) they comprise: the *pounamu*, jades that are the sacred property of the clan chiefs; the rare, sculptured *tiki*; various kinds of mats of which one is called *koruwai* (the only Maori word recalling the Samoan *oloa*, although we have sought for an equivalent). A Maori document gives the name *taonga* to the *karakia*, individual heritable magic spells. *J.P.S.*, IX, 126, 133.

[33] E. Best, 'Forest Lore', in *T.N.Z.I.*, XLII, 449.

[34] We should really discuss here the ideas implied in the interesting Maori expression 'to despise *tahu*'. The main document is Best, 'Maori Mythology', in *J.P.S.*, IX, 113. *Tahu* is a symbolic name for food in general, its personification. 'Do not despise *tahu*' is the injunction to a person who refuses a gift of food. It would take much space to study Maori food beliefs so we simply point out that this personification of food is identical with Rongo, the god of plants and of peace. The association of ideas becomes clearer: hospitality, food, communion, peace, exchange, law.

[35] See Best, 'Spiritual Concepts' in *J.P.S.*, IX, 198.

[36] See Hardeland, *Dayak Wörterbuch* under *indjok*, *irek*, *pahuni*. The comparative study of these institutions could be extended to cover the whole of Malayan, Indonesian and Polynesian civilization. The only difficulty is in recognizing the institution. For instance, it is under the name of 'compulsory trade' that Spencer St. John describes the way in which (in Brunei) the aristocrats seek tribute from the Bisayas by first giving them a present of cloth to be repaid with high interest over a number of years (*Life in the Forests of the Far East*, Vol. II). The error arises from the custom of civilized Malayans of borrowing cultural traits from their less civilized brothers without understanding. We do not enumerate all the Indonesian data on this point.

[37] Not to invite one to a war dance is a sin, a fault which, in the South Island, is called *puha*. H. T. de Croisilles, 'Short Traditions of the South Island' in *J.P.S.*, X, 76. (Note *tahua* means a gift of food.)

Maori ritual of hospitality comprises: an obligatory invitation that should not be refused or solicited; the guest must approach the reception house looking straight ahead; his host should have a meal ready for him straight away and himself partake of it humbly; on leaving, the guest receives a parting gift (Tregear, *The Maori Race*, p. 29). See later, identical rites in Hindu hospitality.

In fact the two rules are closely connected like the gifts they prescribe. Taylor, *Te ika a mani*, p. 132, no. 60, translates a proverb expressing this: 'When raw it is seen, when cooked it is taken' (it is better to eat half-cooked food and to wait until strangers arrive than to have it cooked and be obliged to share it with them).

Chief Hekemaru, according to legend, refused food unless he had been seen and received by the village he was visiting. If his procession passed through unnoticed and then messengers arrived begging him to return and take food, he replied that 'food would not follow his back'. He meant that food offered to the 'sacred back of his head' would endanger those who gave it. Hence the proverb: 'Food will not follow at the back of Hekemaru' (Tregear, *The Maori Race*, p. 79).

[38] Among the tribe of Tuhoe Best ('Maori Mythology' in *J.P.S.*, VIII, 113) saw these principles: When a famous chief is to visit a district, his *mana* precedes him. The people hunt and fish for good food. They get nothing. 'That is because our *mana* has preceded us and driven all the food (fish and birds) afar off that they may not be visible to the people. Our *mana* has banished them.' (There follows an explanation of snow in terms of *whai riri*—a sin against water—which keeps food away from men.) This rather difficult passage describes the condition of the land as the result of a *hapu* of hunters who had failed to make preparations to receive the chief of another clan. They would have committed *kaipapa*, a ' sin against food', and thus destroyed their cultivations, hunting grounds and fisheries—their entire sources of food.

[39] E.g. Arunta, Unmatjera, Kaitish; Spencer and Gillen, *Northern Tribes of Central Australia*, p. 610.

[40] On *vasu* see especially Williams, *Fiji and the Fijians*, 1858, Vol. I, p. 34, and cf. Steinmetz, *Entwickelung für die Strafe*, Vol. II, pp. 241 ff. The right of the sister's son is only analogous to family communism. There are other rights present, the right of in-laws and what may be called 'permitted theft'.

[41] See *Chukchee*. Obligation to give, receive and return gifts and hospitality is more marked with the Maritime than, the Reindeer Chukchee. See 'Social Organization', *J.N.P.E.*, VII, 634, 637. Cf. rules for sacrificing and slaughtering reindeer. 'Religion', ibid., II, 375; the duty of inviting, the right of the guest to demand what he wants and his obligation to give a present.

[42] The obligation to give is a marked Eskimo characteristic. See our 'Variations saisonnières des Sociétés Eskimos' in *A.S.*, IX, 121. A recent work on the Eskimo gives other tales which impart generosity; Hawkes, 'The Labrador Eskimo' in *Canadian Geological Survey*, Anthropological Series, p. 159.

In 'Variations saisonnières' we considered Alaskan Eskimo feasts as a combination of Eskimo elements and potlatch borrowings. But since writing that we have found the true potlatch as well as gift customs described for the Chukchee and Koryak in Siberia, so the Eskimo might have borrowed from them. Also the plausible theory of Sauvageot ('Journal des Américanistes', 1924) on the Asiatic origin of Eskimo languages should be taken into account. This theory confirms the archaeological and anthropological theories on the origin of the Eskimo and their civilization. Everything points to the fact that the western Eskimo are nearer the origin linguistically and ethnologically than the eastern and central. This seems proved by Thalbitzer.

One must then say that the eastern Eskimo have a potlatch of very ancient origin. The special totems and masks of the western festivals are clearly of Indian derivation. The disappearance in east and central Arctic America of the Eskimo potlatch is ill explained except by the gradual degeneration of the eastern Eskimo societies.

⁴³ Hall, *Life with the Esquimaux*, Vol. II, p. 320. It is remarkable that this is found not with reference to the Alaskan potlatch, but to the central Eskimo, who have only communal winter festivals and gift exchange. This shows that the notion extends beyond the limits of the potlatch proper.

⁴⁴ Nelson, 'Eskimos about Behring Straits' in *A.R.B.A.E.*, XVIII, 303, and Porter, *11th Census*, pp. 138, 141, and especially Wrangold *Statistische Ergebnisse*, etc., p. 132. For the 'asking stick', cf. Hawkes, 'The Inviting-in Feast of the Alaskan Eskimos' in *Canadian Geological Survey*, Memo. 45, Anthropological Series, II, 7.

⁴⁵ Hawkes, ibid., pp. 3, 7. Cf. p. 9 description of one such festival, Unalaklit v. Malemiut. One of the most characteristic traits is the series of comical prestations on the first day and the gifts concerned. One tribe tries to make the other laugh and can demand anything it wants. The best dancers receive valuable presents (pp. 12–14). This is a clear and rare example (I know of others in Australia and America) of representation in ritual of a theme which is frequent enough in mythology: the spirit of jealousy which, when it laughs, leaves hold of its object.

The Inviting-in Festival ends with a visit of the *angekok* (shaman) to the spirit-men, *inua*, whose mask he wears and who tell him they have enjoyed the dance and will send game. Cf. the gift made to seals, Jennes, 'Life of the Copper Eskimos' in *Report of the Canadian Arctic Expedition*, Vol. XII, 1922, p. 178.

Other themes of gift-giving customs are strongly marked; e.g. the chief *naskuk* has no right to refuse a gift or food however scarce it may be for fear of being evermore disgraced. Hawkes, ibid., p. 9.

Hawkes rightly considers (p. 19) the festival of the Dene described by Chapman (*Congrès des Américanistes de Québec*, 1907, Vol. II) as an Eskimo borrowing from Indians.

⁴⁶ See illustration in *Chukchee*, p. 403.

⁴⁷ Ibid., pp. 399–401.

⁴⁸ *Koryak*, pp. 64, 90, 98.

⁴⁹ *Chukchee*, p. 400. On customs of this type see Frazer, *The Golden Bough* (3rd edn.), Vol. III, pp. 78–85, 91 ff.; Vol. X, pp. 169 ff., also pp. 1, 161.

⁵⁰ This is a basic trait of all North-West American potlatch. It is not very noticeable, however, since the ritual is so totemistic that its effect upon nature is less evident than its influence over spirits. It is more obvious

in the Behring Straits, especially with the Chukchee and the Eskimo potlatch of Saint-Lawrence Isle.

⁵¹ See potlatch myth in Bogoras, *Chukchee Mythology*, p. 14. One shaman asks another: 'With what will you answer?' (i.e. make return gift). A struggle ensues but finally they come to an agreement; they exchange their magic knives and necklaces, then their (assistant) spirits and lastly their bodies (p. 15). Thereafter they are not entirely successful for they forget to exchange their bracelets and tassels ('my guide in motion'), p. 16. These objects have the same spiritual value as the spirits themselves.

⁵² Jochelsen, 'Koryak Religion', *J.N.P.E.*, VI, 30. A Kwakiutl spirit song (from winter ceremony shamanism) comments:

> 'You send us all things from the other world, O spirits
> You heard that we were hungry
> We shall receive many things from you.'

Sec. Soc., p. 487.

⁵³ *Foi Jurée*, pp. 224 ff., refers.

⁵⁴ Koopen, pp. 163–8, 158–9, 3 and 5 of the summary.

⁵⁵ *Argonauts*, p. 511.

⁵⁶ Ibid., pp. 72, 184.

⁵⁷ Ibid., p. 512. Cf. 'Baloma, Spirits of the Dead', in *J.R.A.I.*, 1917.

⁵⁸ The Maori myth of Te Kanava (Grey, *Polynesian Mythology*, Routledge edn., p. 213) relates how spirits took the shadows of the *pounamu* (jasper, etc.—in other words *taonga*) displayed in their honour. An identical myth from Mangaia (Wyatt Gill, *Myths and Songs from the South Pacific*, p. 257) tells the same tale about red shell necklaces and how they gain the favours of the beautiful Manapu.

⁵⁹ *Argonauts*, p. 513. Malinowski (p. 510, etc.) lays too much claim to the novelty of his data which are identical with aspects of Tlingit and Haida potlatch.

⁶⁰ 'Het Primitieve Denken, voorn. in Pokkengebruiken' in *Bijdr. tot de Taal-, Land-, en Volkenk. v. Nederl. Indie*, LXXI, 245–6.

⁶¹ Crawley, *The Mystic Rose*, p. 386, has already put forward a hypothesis on these lines, and Westermarck examined it and adduced some proof. See especially *History of Human Marriage*, 2nd edn., Vol. I, pp. 394 ff. His approach is vitiated since he identifies the system of total prestations and the more highly developed potlatch in which the exchanges (including exchange of women in marriage) form only a part. On fertility in marriage assured by gifts made to the spouses see later.

⁶² Vajasaneyisamhita. See Hubert and Mauss, 'Essai sur le Sacrifice' in *A.S.*, II. 105.

⁶³ Tremearne, *Haussa Superstitions and Customs*, 1913, p. 55.

⁶⁴ Tremearne, *The Ban of the Bori*, 1915, p. 239.

⁶⁵ Robertson Smith, *Religion of the Semites*, p. 283: the poor are the guests of God.

⁶⁶ The Betsimisaraka of Madagascar tell how of two chiefs one shared out all his possessions and the other kept all of his. God sent fortune to the generous chief and ruined the selfish one (Grandidier, *Ethnographie de Madagascar*, Vol. II, p. 67).

⁶⁷ See Westermarck, *Origin and Development of Moral Ideas*, Vol. I, Chap. XXIII on notions of alms, generosity and liberality.

⁶⁸ Questions tend to pose themselves after one's research is finished, and I have not been able to re-read all the literature. But I have no doubt that we could find many more significant traces of the potlatch in Polynesia, e.g. the display of food, *hakari* (Tregear, *The Maori Race*, p. 113) has many of the same details as the similarly named *hekarai* of the Koita Melanesians. See Seligman, *Melanesians*, pp. 141–5. On the *hakari* see also Taylor, *Te ika a mani*, p. 13; Yeats, *An Account of New Zealand*, 1835, p. 139. Cf. Tregear, *M.C.D.* under *hakari*. Cf. a myth in Grey, *Polynesian Mythology*, p. 189 which describes the *hakari* of Maru, god of war, when the attitude of the recipients is identical with that in New Caledonian, Fijian and New Guinea festivals.

A song collected by Sir E. Grey (*Konga Moteatea, Mythology and Traditions in New Zealand*, 1853, p. 132) has verse 2:

> 'Give me *taonga* from this direction
> Give me *taonga*, that I may place in heaps
> To place them in heaps towards the land
> To place them in heaps towards the sea, etc. . . .
> Give me my *taonga*.'

It is seen how important the notion of *taonga* is to the ritual of the festival. Cf. Percy Smith, 'Wars of the Northern against the Southern Tribes' in *J.P.S.*, VIII, 156.

Even although the potlatch may not exist in present Polynesian society it may well have existed in the civilization overrun and absorbed by the immigration of Polynesians, and the latter themselves may have had it before their migration. There is in fact a good reason why it should have disappeared from a part of the area, for in the islands there is a hierarchy of clans clustered round a monarchy; thus one of the chief conditions of the potlatch is absent: an unstable hierarchy changeable from time to time by the jealousy of chiefs. There are clearer traces with the Maori who have chiefs and where clans are set in rivalry against each other.

See Krämer, *Samoa-Inseln*, Vol. I, p. 375 and index under *ifoga* for destruction of property of the American and Melanesian manner. Perhaps the Maori *nuru*, destruction of property following a misdemeanour, may be studied from this angle. In Madagascar the relationships amongst the Lohateny who trade and may insult or ruin each other also show traces of a former potlatch; Grandidier, *Ethnologie de Madagascar*, Vol. II, pp. 131–3; cf. p. 155.

Chapter II

¹ *Die Stellung der Pygmäenvolker*, 1910. We do not agree with Father Schmidt on this point. See *A.S.*, XII, 65 ff.

² *Andamans*, p. 83. 'Although the natives themselves regarded the objects thus given as being presents, yet when a man gave a present to another he expected that he would receive something of equal value in return, and would be very angry if the return present did not come up to his expectations.'

³ *Andamans*, pp. 73, 81; cf. p. 237. Radcliffe-Brown then observes how unstable the contractual activities are, how they lead to sudden quarrels although the point of the exchange is to dispel them.

⁴ Ibid., p. 237.

⁵ Ibid., p. 81.

⁶ Cf. the *kalduke* and *ngia-ngiampe* with the Narrinyeri and the *yutchin* among the Dieri.

⁷ *Andamans*, p. 237.

⁸ Ibid., pp. 245–6. Radcliffe-Brown produces an excellent sociological theory on these manifestations of solidarity, on the identity of sentiments and the character of the manifestations at once constrained and spontaneous. There is a related problem to which we drew attention in 'Expression obligatoire des Sentiments' in *Journal de Psychologie*, 1921.

⁹ One might mention again the question of money in Polynesia. Axes, jades, *tikis*, cachelot teeth are doubtless to be reckoned no less than shells and crystals as currency.

¹⁰ 'La Monnaie Néo-Calédonienne' in *Revue d'Ethnographie*, 1922, p. 328; on money in funeral ceremonies, p. 322. See also 'La Fête du Pilou en Nouvelle-Calédonie', *Anthropologie*, 1922, pp. 226 ff.

¹¹ Ibid., pp. 236–7; cf. pp. 250–1.

¹² Ibid., p. 247.

¹³ Ibid., p. 263; cf. 'La Monnaie Calédonienne', p. 332.

¹⁴ This resembles Polynesian symbolism. In the Mangaia Islands peace was symbolized by a well-built house with a sound roof in which the gods and the clans might gather; Wyatt Gill, *Myths and Songs of the South Pacific*, p. 294.

¹⁵ Père Lambert, *Mœurs des Sauvages Neo-Calédoniens*, 1900, describes numerous potlatches, one in 1856, on p. 119; series of funeral feasts, pp. 234–5; potlatch on a second burial, pp. 240–6; the humiliation and possible flight of a vanquished chief is the occasion of unreturned gifts and potlatches, p. 53. 'Everyone demands another present in return', p. 116. The return gifts are exposed in the display house, p. 125. Presents on visits are obligatory. They are necessary on marriage, pp. 10, 93–4; they are irrevocable and their return is made 'with usury' especially to the *bengam*, a kind of cousin, p. 215. The *trianda* dance of presents, p. 158.

¹⁶ See 'Kula' in *Man*, July 1920, and *Argonauts*.

¹⁷ Malinowski overrates the novelty of his facts, pp. 313–15. The *kula* is really an inter-tribal potlatch of a kind common enough in Melanesia, to which belong the expeditions of this kind described by Père Lambert in New Caledonia, and the great *Olo-olo* of the Fijians, etc. See Mauss, 'Extension du Potlatch en Mélanésie' in *Anthropologie*, 1920. The meaning of the word *kula* is akin to that of various similar words, e.g. *ulu-ulu*. See *H.M.S.*, Vol. II, pp. 415, 485, and Vol. I, p. 160. In certain aspects the *kula* is less characteristic than the American potlatch, for here the islands are smaller and the societies less strong and wealthy than those off the coast of British Columbia where all the traits of the inter-tribal potlatch are found. There are many international potlatches, e.g. Haida v. Tlingit (Sitka was a common village and Nass River a favourite meeting place);

Kwakiutl v. Bellacoola and Heiltsuq; Haida v. Tsimshian, etc.; this is natural for formal exchanges are normally extended across tribal boundaries. Here as elsewhere they have no doubt blazed new trade-routes as well as following the old ones between wealthy maritime tribes.

[18] *Argonauts*, p. 473. Note the expression of modesty: 'My food left over, take it', referring to the gift of a valuable necklace.

[19] Ibid., pp. 95, 189, 193. It is in order to make himself understood to Europeans that the author, p. 187, counts the *kula* as ' ceremonial barter with deferred payment'. The words payment and barter are both European.

[20] See *Prim. Ec.*

[21] Cf. the rite of *tanarere*, display of expedition gains on the shore of *Muwa*, ibid., pp. 374–5, 391. Cf. *uvalaku* on Dobu, p. 381. The best, i.e. luckiest, business man is named.

[22] *Wawoyla* ritual, ibid., pp. 353–4; magic, pp. 360–3.

[23] Ibid., p. 471. See frontispiece, Pl. LX, etc., and p. 155.

[24] This morality is comparable with the fine paragraphs of the *Nicomachean Ethics* on μεγαλοπρέπεια and ἐλευθερία.

[25] *Note on the principle adopted in discussing the idea of money.* We insist, despite Malinowski's objection ('Primitive Currency', in *Economics Journal*, 1923) on using this term. Malinowski (*Argonauts*, p. 499) protested against misuse and criticized the terminology of Seligman. Malinowski applies the term money to objects serving not only as a medium of exchange, but also as a standard of value. Simiand objected in the same way to the use of the term in this type of society. Both of them are surely right; they take the narrow meaning of the term. In this view there is economic value only when there is money. There is money only when precious objects, condensed wealth or tokens of wealth are made into money—when they are named, impersonalized, detached from any relationships with moral, collective or individual persons other than the authority of the state which mints them. The question is then what arbitrary limit we should impose on the use of the word. The above definition can cover only a secondary type of money —our own.

In all societies preceding those which minted gold, bronze and silver, other things, particularly shells and precious metals, were used as a means of exchange and payment; in some present-day societies the same system holds, and it is this system we are describing. These precious objects differ, it is true, from what we are accustomed to consider as purchasing instruments. Beyond their economic nature they have a mystical nature and are talismans or 'life-givers', as Rivers, Perry and Jackson say. Moreover, they have a very general circulation within a society and between societies, but they are still attached to persons or clans (the first Roman coins were struck by *gentes*), to the individuality of their former possessors and to contracts made between moral beings. There value is still subjective. For instance the strings of pearls used as currency in Melanesia are still valued according to the measure of the person who gives them—*H.M.S.*, Vol. II, p. 527; Vol. I, pp. 64, 71, 101, 160 ff. Cf. the expression *Schulterfaden: Forschungen*, Vol. III, pp. 41 ff.; Vol. I, p. 189; *Hüftschnur*, Vol. I, p. 263. We shall note other examples of these institutions. It is true again that these values are unstable and that they are not of a proper character to be measured and stamped, for instance their value varies according to the number and size of the transactions in which they have taken part. Malinowski shows for instance how *vaygu'a* acquire prestige in the course of their travels. In the same way the North-West American coppers and Samoan mats increase in value at each potlatch.

But in two respects these valuables have the same function as money in our society and consequently deserve to be put at least in the same genus. They have the power to buy and this power can be computed. An American copper is paid for with so many blankets; a *vaygu'a* is worth so many baskets of yams. The idea of number is present although the number is not fixed by a state authority and is variable from one *kula* or potlatch to another. Moreover, this purchasing power is in fact liberating. Although it is recognized only between certain definite individuals, tribes or clans, and only among associates, it is none the less public, official and fixed. Brudo, a friend of Malinowski, and like him long resident in the Trobriands, paid his pearl fishermen in *vaygu'a* as well as in European money or goods at a fixed rate. The passage from one system to the other was made without difficulty.

We hold that mankind made a number of tentative steps. At first it was found that certain things, most of them magical and precious, were by custom not destroyed, and these were endowed with the power to exchange (see Mauss, 'Origine de la Notion de la Monnaie', *Anthropologie*, 1914). In the second stage, mankind having succeeded in making things circulate within the tribe and far outside it found that these purchasing instruments could serve as a means to count wealth and make it circulate. This is the stage we are describing at present. The third stage began in ancient Semitic societies which invented the means of detaching these precious things from groups and individuals and of making them permanent instruments of value measurement—universal, if not entirely rational—for lack of any better system.

Thus we hold there was a form of money consisting, as in Africa and Asia today, of blocks and bars of copper, iron, etc., or cattle as in ancient society or present-day Africa.

[26] *Argonauts*, Pl. XIX. It seems that Trobriand women, like the North-West American 'princesses', serve as a means of displaying wealth, which also 'charms' them. Cf. *Forschungen*, Vol. I, pp. 138, 159, 192.

[27] *Argonauts*, map, p. 82. Cf. 'Kula' in *Man*, 1920, p. 101. Malinowski found no myths or other facts explaining the direction of the movements. A reason would be interesting to discover; for, if the reason were contained in the things themselves tending to return to their point of origin, following some original mythical event, this would be very close to the Maori *hau*.

[28] On this trade and civilization see *Melanesians*, Chaps. XXXIII ff. Cf. *A.S.*, XII, 374; *Argonauts*, p. 96.

[29] *Argonauts*, p. 94.

[30] Ibid., pp. 492, 502.

[31] The remote partner (*murimuri*, cf. *muri*, *Melanesians*, pp. 505, 572) is known to at least one of the series of partners.

[32] See general observations on the ceremony, *Argonauts*, pp. 89–90.

[33] Ibid., p. 504, paired names, cf. pp. 89, 271. See myth, p. 323; the way in which *soulava* is spoken of.

[34] Ibid., p. 512.

[35] Ibid., p. 513.

[36] Ibid., p. 340; commentary, p. 347.

[37] On the use of the conch, ibid., pp. 340, 387, 471, Pl. LXI. The conch is sounded on each transaction, at each solemn moment of the common feast, etc. On the distribution and history of the conch see Jackson, 'Pearls and Shells', University of Manchester Series, 1921.

The use of trumpets, drums, etc., on feasts and contracts is met with in a great number of West African, Bantu, Asiatic, American, Indo-European, etc., societies. It is connected with the legal and economic themes we are discussing, and deserves wide study.

[38] *Argonauts*, p. 340, *mwanita*. Cf. the Kiriwina text of the first two lines, p. 448. This is the name of the long black-banded worm with which spondylus necklaces are identified (p. 340). There follows the spell: 'Come there together; I will make you come there together! Come here together; I will make you come here together! The rainbow appears there; I will make the rainbow appear there! The rainbow appears here; I will make the rainbow appear here!' Malinowski, following the natives, considers the rainbow as a simple omen. It may also refer to the many colours of mother-of-pearl. The expression 'Come here together' relates to the valuable objects that will come together in the course of the contract. 'here' and 'there' are represented simply by the sounds *m* and *w*, and are frequently used in magic.

[39] The word is translated (cf. ibid., p. 449) *munumweynise*, redoubled form of *mwana* or *mwaina* which expresses the 'itching' or 'state of excitement'.

[40] I suppose there must have been a line like this because the author says formally on p. 340 that the principal word of the spell means the state of mind which should befall the partner and cause him to make generous gifts.

[41] A taboo imposed during *kula* and *s'oi* mortuary festivals with a view to being able to collect the necessary amount of food, areca nuts and precious objects. Cf. pp. 347–50. The spell extends also to food.

[42] Names of various necklaces. They are not analysed. The names are made up of *bagi-* which means necklace and various other words. There follow other necklace names of an equally magical nature. This spell is for Sinaketa where necklaces are sought and bracelets left and so necklaces only are mentioned. An identical spell is used in the Kiriwina *kula;* but since bracelets are sought there it is bracelet names that are mentioned.

The end of the spell is interesting but only from the point of view of the potlatch: 'I shall *kula*, I shall rob my *kula;* I shall steal my *kula* (partner); I shall pilfer my *kula*. I shall *kula* so as to make my canoe sink. . . . My fame is like thunder, my steps are like earthquake.' This looks strangely American, and there are analogies in Samoa.

[43] Ibid., p. 345. The end is the same as the one just noted.

[44] *Argonauts*, p. 343. Cf. p. 449.

[45] Ibid., p. 348. This couplet follows a series of lines: 'Thy fury ebbs, it ebbs away. O man of Dobu. . . .' Then follows the same series with 'woman of Dobu'. Dobu women are taboo while Kiriwina women prostitute themselves to the visitors.

[46] Ibid., p. 356. Perhaps this is a myth to account for the directions.

[47] One might use Lévy-Bruhl's term 'participations' which implies confusion and the kinds of identification we are concerned with here.

[48] Ibid., pp. 345 ff.

[49] Ibid., p. 98.

[50] This word might also refer to the old type of boar's tooth currency, p. 353.

[51] The *lebu* custom, p. 319. Cf. Myth, p. 313.

[52] Ibid., p. 359. Of a well-known *vaygu'a* it is said: ' Many men died because of it'. In one case at least (Dobu, p. 356), it seems that the *yotile* is always a *mwali*, a bracelet, the feminine principle in the transaction: 'We do not *kwaypolu* or *pokala* them, they are women.' But in Dobu only bracelets are sought and it may be that the fact has no further significance.

[53] It seems there are several kinds of transactions mixed up here. The *basi* may be a necklace (cf. p. 98) or a bracelet of lesser value. But articles not strictly *kula* may also be given in *basi:* lime spatulae for betel, coarse necklaces, large polished axes (*beku*) (cf. pp. 358, 486) which are also a kind of currency.

[54] Ibid., pp. 157, 359.

[55] Malinowski's book, like Thurnwald's, shows the superior observation of the trained sociologist. Thurnwald, noting similar facts in the *mamoko* (*Forschungen*, Vol. III, p. 40), the *Trostgabe* in Buin, gave a lead in describing facts of this kind.

[56] *Argonauts*, p. 189, cf. Pl. XXXVII. Cf. 'secondary trade', p. 100.

[57] These have the generic name of *wawoyla*, pp. 353–4; cf. pp. 360–1; cf. *woyla*, wooing for *kula* gifts, p. 439. This comes into a spell where all the articles which a future partner might possess are enumerated, and whose 'boiling' will decide the giver in his favour.

[58] This is the usual term; 'presentation goods', ibid., pp. 439, 205, 350. The word *vata'i* is used for the same presents given by the people of Dobu, cf. p. 391. These 'arrival gifts' are enumerated in the spell: 'My lime pot it boils; my comb it boils. . . .' In addition to these generic names there are special names for special gifts. The offerings of food taken by the people on Sinaketa to Dobu (and not vice versa), the pots, mats, etc., are called *pokala*, meaning simply 'offering'. Other *pokala* include the *gugu'a* (personal belongings), p. 501, cf. pp. 270, 313, which the individual takes to try to procure (*pokapokala*, p. 360) his future partner, cf. p. 369. In these societies there is a clear distinction made between articles for personal use and 'properties'—durable things belonging to the family or to general circulation.

[59] E.g. ibid., p. 313, *buna*.

[60] E.g. *kaributu*, pp. 344, 358.

⁶¹ Malinowski was told (ibid., p. 276): 'My partner same as my clansman (*kakaveyogu*)—he might fight me. My real kinsman (*veyogu*), same navel-string, would always side with us.'

⁶² This is expressed in the *kula* formula *mwasila*.

⁶³ The leaders of the expedition and the canoes have precedence.

⁶⁴ The amusing Kasabwaybwayreta myth (p. 322) in which the hero obtains the famous Gumakarakedakeda necklace and leaves all his *kula* companions mentions all these motives. See also myth of Tokosikuna, p. 307.

⁶⁵ Ibid., p. 390. At Dobu, pp. 362, 365, etc.

⁶⁶ On the stone axe trade, see *Melanesians*, pp. 350–3. On the *kortumna*, *Argonauts*, pp. 358, 365; they are usually decorated whalebone spoons, decorated spatulae also used as *basi*.

⁶⁷ *Argonauts*, pp. 486–91. For the distribution of these customs throughout North Massim, see *Melanesians*, p. 584. Descriptions of *walaga*, pp. 594, 603; cf. *Argonauts*, pp. 486–7.

⁶⁸ Ibid., p. 479.

⁶⁹ Ibid., p. 472.

⁷⁰ The manufacture and gift of *mwali* by a brother-in-law is *youlo*, pp. 280, 503.

⁷¹ Ibid., pp. 171 ff.; cf. pp. 98 ff.

⁷² Those concerned with canoe-building, the collection of pots, or the furnishing of food.

⁷³ Ibid., p. 167: 'The whole tribal life is permeated by a constant give and take; every ceremony, every legal and customary act is done to the accompaniment of material gift and counter-gift; wealth, given and taken, is one of the main instruments of social organization, of the power of the chief, of the bonds of kinship and of relationship in law.' Cf. pp. 175–6 *et passim*.

⁷⁴ It may even be identical with *kula*, the partners being the same, p. 193; description of *wasi*, pp. 187–8, cf. Pl. XXXVI.

⁷⁵ The obligation remains in spite of the recent losses and inconveniences sustained by the pearl-fishers, who are obliged to take part in the fishing expedition and lose considerable income in virtue of custom.

⁷⁶ Pls. XXXII, XXXIII.

⁷⁷ *Sagali* means distribution, like the Polynesian *hakari*, ibid., p. 491. Cf. pp. 147–50, 170, 192–3.

⁷⁸ In mortuary feasts especially. Cf. *Melanesians*, pp. 594–603.

⁷⁹ *Argonauts*, p. 175.

⁸⁰ Ibid., p. 323; another term, *kwaypolu*, p. 356.

⁸¹ Ibid., pp. 378–9, 354.

⁸² Ibid., pp. 163, 373. The *vakapula* has subdivisions with their own names, e.g. *vewoulo*, initial gift, and *yomelu*, final gift. This shows the identity with the *kula*. Some of the payments have their own names: *karibudaboda* is the payment to canoe builders and more generally any who work, e.g. in the gardens—specially referring to the final payment after the harvest (*urigubu* in the case of annual gifts of harvest fruits to sister's husband, pp. 63–5, 181) and payment for necklaces, pp. 183, 394. This is also *sousula*

if it is very large (cf. manufacture of spondylus discs, pp. 183, 373). *Youlo* is the payment for manufacturing a bracelet. *Puwayu* is the payment of food given to encourage a team of wood-cutters. Cf. the song p. 129: 'The pig, the coco drinks, the yams are finished, and yet we pull—very heavy!'

The words *vakapula* and *mapula* are different forms of the word *pula*, *vaka-* being apparently the causative prefix. *Mapula* Malinowski translates as 'repayment'. It is generally compared with a poultice for it eases the pain and the tedium of the service rendered, compensates for the loss of an object or secret given away, or of the title or privilege ceded.

⁸³ Ibid., p. 179. Gifts for sexual services are *buwana* or *sebuwana*.

⁸⁴ See preceding notes; in the same way *kabigidoya*, p. 164, is the ceremony of presentation of a new canoe, the people who make it, the action of 'breaking the head of the new canoe', etc., as well as the gifts usuriously proffered. Other terms refer to the location of the canoe, p. 186, gifts of welcome, p. 232, etc.

⁸⁵ *Buna*, big cowrie shell gifts, p. 317.

⁸⁶ *Youlo*, *vaygu'a* given as payment for harvest labour, p. 280.

⁸⁷ Ibid., pp. 186, 426, means apparently any usurious counter-prestation. Another name *ula-ula* stands for simple purchases of magic formulae (*sousula* if the payments or gifts are large, p. 183). *Ula-ula* refers also to presents offered to the dead as well as the living, p. 383.

⁸⁸ Brewster, *Hill Tribes of Fiji*, 1922, pp. 91–2.

⁸⁹ Ibid., p. 191.

⁹⁰ Ibid., pp. 23–6.

⁹¹ *Melanesians*, glossary, p. 754; and pp. 77, 93–4, 109, 204.

⁹² See description of *doa*, ibid., pp. 71, 89, 91.

⁹³ Ibid., pp. 95, 146.

⁹⁴ Money is not the only thing in this system that the tribes of the Gulf of New Guinea call by a word identical to the Polynesian of the same meaning. We have noted the identity of the New Zealand *hakari* and the *hakarai* displays of food which Seligman describes from Metu and Koita—*Melanesians*, pp. 144–5, Pls. XVI–XVIII.

⁹⁵ Note the Mota (Banks Is.) dialect word *tun*, clearly the same as *taonga*, means 'to buy', especially a woman. Codrington, *Melanesian Languages*, pp. 307–8, in the myth of Qat buying the night, translates it 'to buy at a great price'. It is in fact a purchase according to potlatch rules, well attested from this part of Melanesia.

⁹⁶ See document quoted in *A.S.*, XII, 372.

⁹⁷ See especially *Forschungen*, Vol. III, pp. 38–41.

⁹⁸ *Zeitschrift für Ethnologie*, 1922.

⁹⁹ *Forschungen*, Vol. III, Pl. II.

¹⁰⁰ *In Primitive New Guinea*, 1924, p. 294. Holmes' description of intermediate gifts is not good. See *basi* above.

¹⁰¹ *Koopen*. This uncertainty about the words which we translate badly as buying and selling is not confined to the Pacific. We return to this later. We note here that in French *vente* means equally sale and purchase; while in Chinese there is difference in tone only between the words meaning purchase and sale.

102 But note the sale of slaves: *Haida T. and M.*, p. 410.

103 Our survey is necessarily incomplete. We make an abstraction from a large number of tribes, principally the following: (1) Nootka (Wakash and Kwakiutl group), Bella Coola (neighbours); (2) Salish tribes of the Southern coast. Research into the distribution of potlatch should be carried as far south as California. From other points of view it should be noted that the institution is spread through the Penutia and Hoka groups; see for example Powers, 'Tribes of California' in *Contributions to North American Ethnology*, III, 153 (Pomo), p. 238 (Wintun), pp. 303, 311 (Maidu); cf. pp. 247, 325, 332–3, for other tribes, and general observations, p. 411.

Also the institutions and arts we describe here in a few words are in fact of very great complexity, and reveal many curious features no less in the absence of traits than in their occurrence. E.g. pottery is unknown as in the South Pacific.

104 There is much sound documentation on these tribes, many philological observations, and texts in the original and translations. See summary in *Foi Jurée*, pp. 21, 171, 215. Main additions are as follows: F. Boas and G. Hunt, in *Eth. Kwa.*; Boas, *Tsim. Myth.*, 1916, pub. 1923. These sources, however, have a disadvantage. The older ones are scarce, and the newer in spite of their depth of detail are not specific from our point of view. Boas and his collaborators in the Jesup Expedition were interested in material culture, language and mythology. Even the oldest works of professional ethnologists (Krause and Jacobsen) or the more recent works of Sapir, Hill Tout, etc., have the same bias. Legal, economic and demographic analysis remain incomplete. Social morphology has been begun by the various censuses of Alaska and British Columbia. M. Barbeau promises a complete monograph on the Tsimshian. For many points on law and economics, see old documents, those of Russian travellers, Krause (*Tlinkit Indianer*), Dawson mainly in the *Bulletin of the Geological Survey of Canada* and the *Proceedings of the Royal Society of Canada*; Swan (Nootka), 'Indians of Cape Flattery' in *Smithsonian Contributions to Knowledge*, 1870; Mayne, *Four Years in British Columbia*, 1862—these are still the best accounts and their dates make them authoritative.

There is a difficulty in the nomenclature of the tribes. The Kwakiutl are one tribe but give their name to several federated tribes, the whole forming a nation of this name. Unless otherwise stated we mean by Kwakiutl the real Kwakiutl tribe. The word itself means 'rich' and is itself an indication of the importance of the economic facts we shall describe.

105 See Emmons, 'The Chilkat Blanket' in *Memoires* of the A.M.N.H., Vol. III.

106 See Rivet, in Meillet and Cohen, *Langues du Monde*, pp. 616 ff. Sapir, in 'Na-Dene Languages', *American Anthropologist*, 1915, reduced Tlingit and Haida to branches of the Athabascan group.

107 On these see *Foi Jurée*, pp. 300–5. For Melanesia see examples in Codrington, *Melanesian Languages*, pp. 106 ff.; Rivers, *H.M.S.*, Vol. I, pp. 70 ff.

108 This word is to be read in both its real and figurative meanings. Just as the Vedic *vajapeya* ritual includes the rite of climbing a ladder,

Melanesian ritual consists in mounting the young chief on a platform. The North-West Coast Snahnaimuq and Shushwap have a scaffolding from which the chief distributes his potlatch; Boas, *5th Report*, p. 39; *9th Report*, p. 459. The other tribes only have a platform on which chiefs and functionaries sit.

[109] Which is how the old authors, Mayne, Dawson, Krause, etc., describe it. See Krause, *Tlinkit Indianer*, pp. 187 ff., for a collection of old documents.

[110] If the hypothesis of linguists is correct and the Tlingit and Haida are simply Athabascans who have adopted the civilization of the North-West (Boas himself is inclined to agree) the 'worn' character of Tlingit and Haida potlatch would be explained. Maybe the violence of North-West American potlatch is accountable by the fact that this civilization is at the point of contact of two groups of families that both had the institution: one from the south of California, the other from Asia.

[111] *Foi Jurée*, pp. 247 ff.

[112] On the potlatch Boas has written nothing better than this extract from the *12th Report*, 1898, pp. 681–2.

'The economic system of the Indians of British Columbia is largely based on credit, just as much as that of civilized communities. In all his undertakings, the Indian relies on the help of his friends. He promises to pay them for this help at a later date. If the help furnished consists in valuables, which are measured by the Indians by blankets as we measure them by money, he promises to pay the amount so loaned with interest. The Indian has no system of writing, and therefore, in order to give security to the transaction, it is performed publicly. The contracting of debts, on the one hand, and the paying of debts, on the other, is the potlatch. This economic system has developed to such an extent that the capital possessed by all the individuals of the tribe combined exceeds many times the actual amount of cash that exists; that is to say, the conditions are quite analogous to those prevailing in our community: if we want to call in all our outstanding debts, it is found that there is not by any means money enough in existence to pay them, and the result of an attempt of all the creditors to call in their loans results in disastrous panic, from which it takes the community a long time to recover.

'It must be clearly understood that an Indian who invites all his friends and neighbours to a great potlatch, and apparently squanders all the accumulated results of long years of labour, has two things in his mind which we cannot but acknowledge as wise and worthy of praise. His first object is to pay his debts. This is done publicly and with much ceremony, as a matter of record. His second object is to invest the fruits of his labours so that the greatest benefit will accrue from them for himself as well as for his children. The recipients of gifts at this festival receive these as loans, which they utilize in their present undertakings, but after the lapse of several years they must repay them with interest to the giver or to his heirs. Thus the potlatch comes to be considered by the Indians as a means of insuring the well-being of their children if they should be left orphans while still young.'

By substituting for Boas's terms words like 'gifts made and returned' (which Boas does use eventually) one sees clearly the function of credit in the potlatch.

On the notion of honour, see Boas, *7th Report*, p. 57.

¹¹³ *Tlingit*, p. 421.

¹¹⁴ It has gone unnoticed that the notion of credit is not only as old but also as simple—or if one prefers as complex—as the notion of direct sale.

¹¹⁵ 'Etude sur les Contrats de l'Epoque de la Première Dynastie Baby-lonienne' in *Nouvelle Revue de l'Histoire du Droit*, 1910, p. 177.

¹¹⁶ *Foi Jurée*, p. 207.

¹¹⁷ Distribution of one's entire property, Kwakiutl, *Sec. Soc.*, p. 469. At initiation of a novice, ibid., p. 551. Koskimo, Shushwap, redistribution, *7th Report*, p. 91. *Tlingit*, p. 442: 'He has spent so much money to let the people see them (his nephews)'. Redistribution of everything won at gambling, *Tlingit T. and M.*, p. 139.

¹¹⁸ On the war of property, see song of Maa, *Sec. Soc.*, pp. 507, 602. 'We fight with property.' The themes of opposition, the war of wealth and real war are found in speeches made at the same potlatch in 1895 at Port Rupert. See Boas and Hunt, in *Kwa. T.*, I, pp. 482, 485; cf. *Sec. Soc.*, pp. 668–73.

¹¹⁹ See specially the myth of Haiyas (*Haida Texts*, VI, no. 83) who loses face at gambling and dies of it. His sisters and nephews mourn and give a potlatch of vengeance which resuscitates him.

¹²⁰ This is the place to study gambling which even with us is not con-sidered contractual but rather as comprised of situations in which honour is engaged and where property is surrendered although it is not absolutely necessary to do so.

Gambling is a form of potlatch and a part of the gift system. It has a wide distribution in North-West America. It is known to the Kwakiutl (*Eth. Kwa.*, p. 1394, *ebayu*: dice *lepa*, p. 1435, cf. *lep*, p. 1448; second potlatch, dance; cf. p. 1423, *maqwacte*) but seems not to play a role comparable with that among the Haida, Tlingit and Tsimshian. The latter are inveterate gamblers. See description of tip-cat among the Haida: *Haida*, pp. 58 ff., 141 ff. for illustration and vocabulary; the same game among the Tlingit: *Tlingit*, p. 443. The Tlingit *naq*, the winning piece, is the same as the Haida *djil*.

Histories have many legends of gambling and stories of chiefs who have lost everything by it. A Tsimshian chief loses even his children (*Tsim. Myth.*, p. 207). A Haida legend recounts the story of a gambling game between Tsimshian and Haida; see *Haida T. and M.*, pp. 843, 847. Etiquette demands that the winner allows freedom to the loser, his wife and children; *Tlingit T. and M.*, p. 137. Note the link with some Asiatic legends. There are undoubted Asiatic influences here. On the distribution of Asiatic games of chance in America see E. B. Tylor's fine 'On American Lot-Games, as Evidence of Asiatic Intercourse' in *Festschrift* to Bastian, 1896, pp. 55 ff.

¹²¹ Davy describes the themes of defiance and rivalry; we add that of the wager. See, e.g. Boas, *Indianische Sagen*, pp. 203–6. Cf. p. 363 for types

of wager. In our days the wager is a survival, and although it engages only honour and credit, it is still a means of the circulation of wealth.

[122] On the destructive potlatch see *Foi Jurée*, p. 224. We add the following comments. To give is to destroy (cf. *Sec. Soc.*, p. 334). Some rites of giving imply destruction—the rite of reimbursing the dowry, or, as Boas says, the marriage debt, includes the rite of 'sinking the canoe' (ibid., pp. 518, 520). Visits to Haida and Tsimshian potlatches entail destruction of the visitors' canoes, then on departure the hosts hand over specially fine canoes of their own (*Tsim. Myth.*, p. 338).

Destruction seems to be a superior form of expenditure. It is called 'killing property' among the Tsimshian and Tlingit (ibid., p. 334; *Tlingit*, p. 442). The same name is given also to the distribution of blankets: 'So my blankets were lost to see him'; ibid., p. 442.

There are two other motifs in destruction at potlatch: first the theme of war: the potlatch is a war and has the name of 'war dance' among the Tlingit (ibid., p. 458, cf. p. 436). As in war, masks, names and privileges of the slain owner may be seized, so in the war of property, property is 'slain'—either one's own so that others may not get it, or that of others by means of giving them goods which they will be obliged, and possibly unable, to repay. The other motif is that of sacrifice. If property can be 'killed' this means it must be 'alive'. A herald says: 'Let our property remain alive (under the attacks) of the reckless chief, let our copper remain unbroken'; *Eth. Kwa.*, p. 1285. Perhaps the meanings of the word *yaq*, to lie dead, to distribute a potlatch, can be thus explained (*Kwa. T.*, I, 59, and *Eth. Kwa.*, index).

As in normal sacrifice the things destroyed are transmitted to the clan ancestors. This is developed among the Tlingit (*Tlingit*, pp. 443, 462) whose ancestors not only are present at the potlatch but profit from presents given to their living namesakes. Destruction by fire is characteristic. For the Tlingit see interesting myth, *Tlingit T. and M.*, p. 82. Haida, sacrifice by fire, *Haida T. and M.*, pp. 28, 31, 91. The theme is less evident among the Kwakiutl for whom, nevertheless, there is a great divinity called 'Sitting-on-Fire' and to whom sacrifice is made, among other things, of the clothing of sick children to pay him: *Eth. Kwa.*, pp. 705–6.

[123] *Sec. Soc.*, p. 353.

[124] It seems that even the words 'exchange' and 'sale' are lacking in the Kwakiutl language. In Boas' glossaries I found the word sale only with reference to the sale of a copper; but the bidding entailed is nothing less than a sale—a kind of generosity match. Exchange I found under the word *l'ay*, but in the text, *Kwa. T.*, I, p. 77, it is used only with reference to a change of name.

[125] See the expression 'greedy for food', *Eth. Kwa.*, p. 1462; 'desirous to get wealth quickly', ibid., p. 1394; note the imprecation against 'small chiefs'—'the little ones who deliberate; the little hard-struggling ones, the little ones whom you have vanquished, who promise to give away canoes, the little ones to whom property is given . . . the little ones who work secretly for property . . . the little traitors . . .' (Property translates *maneq*, return of a favour, p. 1403). Ibid., p. 1287, for another speech where it is

said of a chief who has given a potlatch, and of his people who receive but do not give away: 'It is only said he satisfied their hunger. It is only said he made them vomit. . . . It is just said he put them across his back'; ibid., p. 1293.

One need not consider this as being bad economics, or that it is simply a kind of laziness based on community in family life. The Tsimshian condemn avarice and tell of their hero Crow (the creator) how he was sent away by his father because he was greedy; *Tsim. Myth.*, p. 260.

[126] 'Injuria', *Mélanges Appleton;* 'Magie et Droit Individuel', *A.S.*, X, 28.

[127] One pays for the honour of dancing, among the Tlingit (*Tlingit T. and M.*, p. 141). There is payment to a chief who composes a dance. Among the Tsimshian Boas says that everything is done on account of honour, and the wealth and display of vanity is outstanding; *5th Report*, p. 19. Duncan, in Mayne, *Four Years in British Columbia*, p. 265, says: 'for the sheer vanity of it'. Much ritual—not only that of climbing—refers to this, e.g. that of 'lifting the coppers' among the Kwakiutl (*Kwa. T.*, I, p. 499); 'lifting the spear' (*Tlingit T. and M.*, p. 117); 'lifting the potlatch pole', the house-beam and the greasy pole. It should not be forgotten that the purpose of the potlatch is to see which is the 'highest' family (cf. comments of chief Katishan on the myth of Crow, *Tlingit T. and M.*, p. 119).

[128] Tregear, *M.C.D.*, under *mana*. Here one might study the notion of wealth. From one point of view the rich man is one who has *mana* in Polynesia, *auctoritas* in Rome and who, in North-West America, is 'large' —*walas* (*Eth. Kwa.*, p. 1396). All that is required is to show the connection between the notion of wealth, that of authority—the right to control those to whom one gives—and the potlatch; and it is clear enough. E.g. among the Kwakiutl one of the most important clans is the Walasaka (which is the name of a family, a dance and a fraternity). The name means 'the great ones who come from above', who distribute potlatch: *walasila* means not only wealth but also 'distribution of blankets on the occasion of the sale of a copper'. Another metaphor states that a man is made 'heavy' by a potlatch given, *Sec. Soc.*, pp. 558–9. The chief is said to 'swallow the tribes' to which he distributes his wealth; he 'vomits property', etc.

[129] A Tlingit song says of the Crow Phratry: 'You are the ones that made the Wolf Phratry valuable' (*Tlingit T. and M.*, p. 398). In the two tribes the principle is clear that the respect and honour one should give ought to be in the form of gifts. *Tlingit*, p. 451.

[130] The etiquette concerning the unsolicited gift, to be received with dignity, is well marked in these tribes. There are instructive Tsimshian, Kwakiutl and Haida facts: at feasts, chiefs and nobles eat little while vassals and commoners gorge themselves: *Kwakiutl*, pp. 427, 430. Dangers in eating much, *Tsim. Myth.*, pp. 59, 149, 153; singing at the feast, *Kwakiutl*, pp. 430, 437. The conch shell is blown so it will be known they are not starving, *Kwa. T.*, I, p. 486. The noble never solicits; the shaman never asks for payment, his 'spirit' protects him; *Eth. Kwa.*, pp. 731, 742; *Haida T. and M.*, pp. 238–9. Among the Kwakiutl, however, there is a dance of 'mendacity'.

[131] Tlingit and Haida potlatch has this principle well developed: *Tlingit*, pp. 443, 462. Note discourse in *Tlingit T. and M.*, p. 373. The spirits smoke along with the guests. Cf. p. 385: 'Here for you . . . we are dancing not we it is we are dancing. Long ago died our uncles it is who are dancing here.' The guests are spirits, luck-bearers, *gona' qadet* (ibid., p. 119). We have here a confusion of the two things, sacrifice and gift, comparable with the cases we have so far cited (except perhaps the effect upon nature). To give to the living is to give to the dead. A notable Tlingit tale (*Tlingit T. and M.*, p. 227) states that a resuscitated individual knows if a potlatch is given for him; and the theme that spirits reproach the living for not giving a potlatch is common. The Kwakiutl have the same ideas; see e.g. a speech in *Eth. Kwa.*, p. 788. The living with the Tsimshian represent the dead; Tate writes to Boas: 'In some of these cases offerings appear rather in the form of presents given at a feast': *Tsim. Myth.*, p. 452. Page 846 for comparison with Haida, Tlingit and Tsimshian.

[132] Well described in Krause, *Tlinkit Indianer*, p. 240.

[133] *Foi Jurée*, pp. 171 ff., 251 ff. Tsimshian and Haida forms are similar although the clan is more in evidence in the former.

[134] There is no need to restate Davy's demonstration of the relationship between the potlatch and political status, particularly that of the son-in-law and son. Nor is it necessary to note the solidarity value of the feasts and exchanges. E.g. the exchange of canoes by two spirits means that they have 'but one heart', the one being the father, the other the son-in-law; *Sec. Soc.*, p. 387. In *Kwa. T.*, I, p. 274, is added: 'It was as if they had exchanged names.' Also ibid., p. 23: in a Nimkish mythical feast (another Kwakiutl tribe) the aim of the marriage feast is to instal the girl in the village where she will eat for the first time.

[135] The funeral potlatch has been seen and studied for the Haida and the Tlingit; with the Tsimshian it is connected with the end of mourning, at an erection of the totem pole and with cremation; *Tsim. Myth.*, pp. 534 ff. Boas makes no mention of funeral potlatch for the Kwakiutl although it is referred to in a myth: *Kwa. T.*, I, p. 407.

[136] Potlatch to retain one's right to an emblem: *Haida*, p. 107. See story of Legek, *Tsim. Myth.*, p. 386. Legek is the name of the principal Tsimshian chief. Also ibid., p. 364—stories of chief Nesbalas, another great Tsimshian, and how he made fun of chief Haimas. One of the most important Kwakiutl chiefly titles, Lewikilaq, is Dabend (*Kwa. T.*, I, p. 19; cf. *dabendgala*, *Eth. Kwa.*, p. 1406) who before the potlatch has a name meaning 'unable to hold firm' and after the potlatch takes this name which means 'able to hold firm'.

[137] A Kwakiutl chief says: 'This is my pride, the names of the root of my family, for all my ancestral chiefs gave away property' (*Eth. Kwa.*, p. 887, cf. p. 843).

[138] 'Therefore I am covered in property. Therefore I am rich. Therefore I am a counter of property', *Eth. Kwa.*, p. 1280.

[139] To buy a copper is to put it 'beneath the name of' the buyer: *Sec. Soc.*, p. 345. Another metaphor states that the name of the giver of the potlatch takes on weight by giving it; ibid. Other expressions denote the

superiority of the giver over the donee. There is the notion that the latter is a sort of slave until he ransoms himself. The Haida say 'the name is bad' —*Haida*, p. 70; the Tlingit say that one puts gifts 'on the backs' of the people who receive them—*Tlingit*, p. 428. The Haida have two suggestive phrases: to make one's needle 'go' or 'run quickly', meaning apparently to fight an inferior: *Haida*, p. 162.

¹⁴⁰ See story of Haimas, how he loses his liberty, privileges, masks, his auxiliary spirits, family and property; *Tsim. Myth.*, pp. 361–2.

¹⁴¹ *Eth. Kwa.*, p. 805; Hunt, Boas's Kwakiutl informant, writes: 'I do not know why the chief . . . Maxuyalidze (i.e. potlatch-giver) never gave a feast. That is all about this. He is called *q'elsem* (that is "rotten face"), one who gives no feast.'

¹⁴² In fact the potlatch is a dangerous thing if one receives from it or if one does not give one. People attending a mythical potlatch died of it (*Haida Texts*, p. 626; cf. p. 667, same myth from the Tsimshian). Comparisons in Boas, *Indianische Sagen*, p. 356. It is dangerous to participate in the food of one who gives a potlatch or to take part in a potlatch of the spirits in the world below. See a Kwakiutl (Awikenoq) legend, ibid., p. 329. See also the fire myth of Crow who draws food from his flesh: Ctatloq, ibid., p. 76; Nootka, ibid., p. 106. Cf. *Tsim. Myth.*, pp. 694–5.

¹⁴³ Potlatch is a game and a trial; e.g. a trial consists in not hiccuping during the feast—rather die than that, they say. *Kwakiutl*, p. 428. See a form of challenge: 'Let us try to have (our dishes) emptied by our guests' (*Eth. Kwa.*, p. 991). There is no clear distinction between the meanings 'to give food', 'to return food' and 'to take vengeance' (ibid., glossary under *yenesa* and *yenka*).

¹⁴⁴ We noted above the equivalence of potlatch and war. A knife on the end of a stick is a symbol of the Kwakiutl potlatch, *Kwa. T.*, I, p. 483. With the Tlingit it is a raised spear (*Tlingit T. and M.*, p. 117). See Tlingit potlatch compensation rites: war of the people of Kloo against the Tsimshian, ibid., pp. 432–3; dances of enslavement; and a potlatch without dancing, for a case of murder.

¹⁴⁵ Ritual faults of the Kwakiutl: see *Sec. Soc.*, pp. 433, 507. Expiation consists of giving a potlatch or at least a gift.

This is a most important point in all these societies. Distribution of wealth has the role of payment of a fine or propitiation of spirits and re-establishment of solidarity between spirits and men. Père Lambert, *Mœurs des Sauvages Neo-Calédoniens*, p. 66, noted with the Kanak the right of uterine relatives to indemnity if one of them loses blood in his father's family. Among the Tsimshian it is exactly the same: Duncan, in Mayne, *Four Years in British Columbia*, p. 264, cf. p. 296. The Maori *muru* is probably comparable.

Potlatch for the ransom of captives is to be interpreted in the same way. It is not only to regain its captured members but also to re-establish the 'name' that the family gives a potlatch. See story of Dzebasa, *Tsim. Myth.*, p. 388. The Tlingit have the same: Krause, *Tlinkit Indianer*, p. 245; Porter, *11th Census*, p. 54; *Tlingit*, p. 449.

Kwakiutl potlatches to expiate ritual faults are common. Note potlatch of expiation for parents of twins who are going to work, *Eth. Kwa.*, p. 691. A potlatch is due to your father-in-law to regain a wife who has left you; see glossary, ibid., p. 1423. If a chief wants an occasion to give a potlatch he may send his wife back to her father as a pretext; *5th Report*, p. 42.

¹⁴⁶ A long list of these obligations, at feasts, after fishing, collecting fruits, hunting or opening preserved food is given in *Eth. Kwa.*, pp. 757 ff. Cf. p. 607 for etiquette.

¹⁴⁷ See *Tsim. Myth.*, pp. 439, 512; cf. p. 534 for payment of services. Kwakiutl example: payment to keeper of blankets, *Sec. Soc.*, pp. 614, 629.

¹⁴⁸ Payments to relatives: *Tsim. Myth.*, p. 534; cf. *Foi Jurée*. p. 196, for opposed systems among Tlingit and Haida, and division of potlatch by families.

¹⁴⁹ A Masset Haida myth (*Haida Texts*, X, pt. 2, no. 43) recounts how an old chief does not give enough potlatches; others leave off inviting him, he dies of it, his nephews make an image of him and give ten feasts in his name, and he is born again. In another myth, ibid., p. 722, a spirit addresses a chief: 'Thy property is too much. Potlatch very soon.' He builds a house and pays the builders. In another myth, ibid., p. 723, a chief says: 'I will not keep a part of the property for myself.' And later: 'I will potlatch ten times.'

¹⁵⁰ On the manner in which the clans regularly confront each other see *Sec. Soc.*, p. 343 and *Tsim. Myth.*, p. 497. In phratry societies this naturally happens; cf. *Haida*, p. 162; *Tlingit*, p. 424. The principle is shown well in the myth of Crow, *Tlingit T. and M.*, p. 115.

¹⁵¹ The Tlingit have a remarkable expression: guests are said to 'float', their canoes 'wander about on the sea', the totem pole they bring is 'adrift'; and it is the invitation to the potlatch that halts them (*Tlingit T. and M.*, pp. 394–5). One of the common titles of Kwakiutl chiefs is 'Towards whom one paddles', 'The Place where one comes'; e.g. *Eth. Kwa.*, p. 187.

¹⁵² The offence of neglecting someone means that the relatives abstain from attending the potlatch. In a Tsimshian myth the spirits do not come if the Great Spirit is not invited; *Tsim. Myth.*, p. 277. A story tells how the great chief Nesbalas was not invited and the other Tsimshian chiefs stayed away, ibid., p. 357.

Note the frequent assertion—common also in European and Asiatic folklore—of the danger in not inviting orphans, foundlings and poor relatives, e.g. *Indianische Sagen*, pp. 301, 303; *Tsim. Myth.*, pp. 292, 295, where a beggar is the totem or totemic god. Cf. Boas, ibid., pp. 784 ff.

Of course one does not invite those who do not give feasts or who have no feast names: *Eth. Kwa.*, p. 707. Those who do not return a potlatch, ibid., glossary under *waya* and *wayapo lela*.

The offence also has political consequences, e.g. a Tlingit potlatch with Athabascans from the East: *Tlingit*, p. 435; cf. *Tlingit T. and M.*, p. 117.

¹⁵³ *Tsim. Myth.*, pp. 170–1.

¹⁵⁴ Actually Boas puts this sentence from Tate's text in a note but the moral of the myth should not be separated from the myth itself.

¹⁵⁵ Cf. Tsimshian myth of Negunaks, ibid., p. 287 and notes p. 846.

[156] E.g. the invitation to the blackcurrant feast; the herald says: 'We come back to call you, the only one (who has not come yet)'; *Eth. Kwa.*, p. 752.

[157] *Sec. Soc.*, p. 543.

[158] With the Tlingit, guests who have waited two years before coming to a potlatch to which they had been invited are 'women'. *Tlingit T. and M.*, p. 119.

[159] *Sec. Soc.*, p. 345. With the Kwakiutl one is obliged to attend the whale feast although the oil may make one sick: *Eth. Kwa.*, p. 1046; cf. p. 1048, 'try to eat everything'.

[160] Thus sometimes guests are invited in fear, for should they reject the invitation they would be showing themselves superior. A Kwakiutl chief tells a Koskimo chief (same nation): 'Do not refuse my friendly invitation as I will be ashamed, do not reject my wishes. . . . I am not one of those that pretend, that give only to those that will buy (i.e. will give). There, my friend.' *Sec. Soc.*, p. 546.

[161] Ibid., p. 355.

[162] See *Eth. Kwa.*, p. 774 for another description of the oil and salal berry feast; it is Hunt's and appears to be very good; it seems also that this ritual is employed when one is giving out neither invitations nor gifts. A rite of the same kind to spite a rival has songs and drumming (ibid., p. 770) as with the Eskimo.

[163] A Haida phrase is: 'You do the same. Show me some good food.' *Haida Texts*, X, 685; Kwakiutl, *Eth. Kwa.*, pp. 738, 767; p. 770 story of Polelasa.

[164] Songs of dissatisfaction, *Tlingit T. and M.*, p. 396, nos. 26, 29.

[165] Tsimshian chiefs usually send a messenger to examine presents brought by potlatch guests: *Tsim. Myth.*, p. 184, cf. pp. 430, 434. According to a capitulary of the year 803 there was a similar functionary at the court of Charlemagne.

[166] The Tlingit myth of Crow tells how he is absent from a feast because the opposite phratry is noisy and has overstepped the centre line which, in the dancing house, should separate them. Crow fears they are invincible; *Tlingit T. and M.*, p. 118. The inequality resulting from acceptance is well shown in Kwakiutl discourses: *Sec. Soc.*, pp. 355, 667, 669.

[167] E.g. *Tlingit*, pp. 440–1.

[168] With the Tlingit a ritual enables a host to force upon his guest acceptance of his gift. The dissatisfied guest makes a show of departing. The host offers him double and mentions the name of a dead relative; *Tlingit*, p. 442. This is probably connected with the quality which the parties have of representing their ancestral spirits.

[169] *Eth. Kwa.*, p. 1281: 'The chiefs of the tribes never return (feasts) . . . they disgrace themselves, and you rise as head chief over those who have disgraced themselves.'

[170] See speech on the potlatch of the great chief Legek, *Tsim. Myth.*, p. 386. The Haida are told: 'You shall be the last one among the chiefs, for you are not able to throw away coppers like the high chief has done.'

[171] The ideal is to give a potlatch which is not returned. Cf. 'You wish to give away property that is not to be returned'; *Eth. Kwa.*, p. 1282. One who has given a potlatch is compared to a tree or a mountain: 'I am the only great tree, I the chief. You here are right under me. . . . You surround me like a fence. . . . I am the first to give you property'—ibid., p. 1290. 'Raise the unattainable potlatch-pole, for this is the only thick tree, the only thick root.' The Haida use a spear metaphor. Those who accept 'live on the chief's spear'—*Haida Texts*, p. 486.

[172] Note the story of an insult for a bad potlatch, *Tsim. Myth.*, p. 314. The Tsimshian never forget the two coppers owing to them by the Wutsenaluk, ibid., p. 364.

[173] The name remains 'broken' so long as a copper of equivalent value to that of the challenge is not broken; *Sec. Soc.*, p. 543.

[174] When a man thus discredited borrows the means to make a necessary redistribution, he is said to 'pledge his name' or to 'sell a slave'; *Sec. Soc.*, p. 341; cf. *Eth. Kwa.*, p. 1451; p. 1424 under *kelgelgend;* cf. p. 1420.

[175] Peace ritual of the Haida, Tsimshian and Tlingit consists of prestations with immediate counter-prestations—exchanges of decorated coppers and hostages—women and slaves. E.g. in the Tsimshian war against the Haida (*Haida T. and M.*, p. 395): 'They had women on each side marry the opposites, because they feared they would be angry again. Now there was peace.' In a Haida-Tlingit war there is a compensation potlatch, p. 396.

[176] *Tsim. Myth.*, pp. 511–12.

[177] (*Kwakiutl*): a property distribution in both directions. Boas, *Sec. Soc.*, p. 418; repayment the following year of fines for ritual faults, p. 596; usurious repayment of bridewealth, ibid., pp. 365–6, 518–20, 563.

[178] The Tsimshian language distinguishes between the *yaok*, the great inter-tribal potlatch (*Tsim. Myth.*, p. 537; cf. pp. 511, 968; wrongly translated as 'potlatch') and the others. Haida distinguishes between *walgal* and *sitka* (*Haida*, pp. 35, 68, 178–9—funerary and other potlatches). The common Kwakiutl and Chinook word *pola* (to seize) seems to mean not potlatch so much as the feast or its effect (*Kwa. T.*, I, p. 211). *Polas* means the man who gives a feast (*Kwa. T.*, II, pp. 43, 79) and also the place where one is seized (legend of the title of one of the Dzawadaenoxu chiefs). Cf. *Eth. Kwa.*, p. 770. The commonest word in Kwakiutl is *p'es*, to flatten (a rival's name)—*Eth. Kwa.*, glossary. The inter-tribal potlatches seem to have a special name, *maxwa* (*Kwa. T.*, I, p. 451); somewhat improbably Boas derives from the root *ma* two other words, *mawil*, initiation room, and the name for the orc (*Eth. Kwa.* glossary). In fact Kwakiutl has a number of technical terms for all kinds of potlatch, payments and repayments (or rather gifts and counter-gifts), on marriages, to shamans, for advances, unpaid interest, etc.; e.g. *men(a)*, pick up, *Eth. Kwa.*, p. 218, a small potlatch in which a girl's clothing is thrown to the people for them to pick up: *payol*, to give a copper; there is a different term for giving a canoe; ibid., p. 1448. The terms are numerous, unstable and overlapping.

[179] See Barbeau, 'Le Potlatch', *Bulletin de la Société Géographique de Québec*, 1911, p. 278.

[180] In Tsimshian the distinction between property and possessions is very clear. In *Tsim. ·Myth.*, Boas says: 'While the possession of what is called rich food was essential for maintaining the dignity of the family, the provisions themselves were not counted as constituting wealth. Wealth is obtained by selling provisions for other kinds of goods, which, after they have been accumulated, are distributed in the potlatch.'—p. 435.

Kwakiutl distinguish in the same way between simple provisions and property-wealth. Property and wealth are equivalent. Property has two terms: *yäq* or *yàq; Eth. Kwa.*, glossary, p. 1393 (cf. *yàqu*, to distribute). This word has two derivatives, *yeqala*, property, and *yaxulu*, talismans, paraphernalia; cf. words derived from *yä*, ibid., p. 1406. The other word is *dadekas*, cf. *Kwa. T.*, I, p. 519, cf. p. 433; in Newettee dialect, *daoma*, *dedemala* (*Eth. Kwa.*, glossary). The root of this word is *da*. The meaning of this root is curiously like that of the identical Indo-European radical meaning to receive, take, accept in hand, handle, etc. Of the derived words one means 'to take a piece of one's enemy's clothing to bewitch him', and the other 'to take in one's hand', 'to put in the house' (see later on meanings of *manus* and *familia*), with reference to blankets given in advance for the purchase of coppers, to be returned with interest; another word means 'to put blankets on one's adversary's heap'. An even stranger derivative is *dadeka*, 'to be jealous of each other' (*Kwa. T.*, I, p. 133). Clearly the original meaning must be: the thing which one takes and which makes one jealous; cf. *dadego*, to fight—doubtless to fight with property.

Other words have the same meanings, but more precisely, e.g. *mamekas*, property in the house, *Kwa. T.*, I, p. 169.

[181] *Eth. Kwa.*, pp. 706 ff. There is hardly anything morally and materially valuable (we purposely do not say 'useful') which is not subject to beliefs of this kind. 'Moral' things are goods and property which are the object of gifts and exchanges. E.g. just as in more primitive civilisations, such as the Australian, so with the Tlingit; after the potlatch one 'leaves' a dance in exchange to those who gave the potlatch—*Tlingit*, p. 442. The Tlingit property which is most inviolable and gives rise to the greatest jealousy is the name and the totemic emblem, ibid., p. 416; these it is which make one happy and rich.

Totemic emblems, feasts and potlatches, names won in potlatches, presents which others must return to you as a result of potlatches given, these all follow. E.g. Kwakiutl: 'And now my feast goes to him' (meaning son-in-law)—*Sec. Soc.*, p. 356.

With the Tsimshian decorated dance and parade masks and hats are called 'a certain amount of property following the amount given at a potlatch' (following gifts made by maternal aunts of the chief to the 'women of the tribe'): *Tsim. Myth.*, p. 541.

Inversely, as with the Kwakiutl, things are conceived in moral terms, especially precious objects like essential talismans, the 'giver of death' (*lalayu*), the 'water of life'—these are apparently quartz crystals—blankets, etc. In a curious Kwakiutl saying they are identified with the grandfather: naturally enough, since they are given to the son-in-law only to be transmitted later to the grandson: *Sec. Soc.*, p. 507.

[182] The myth of Djilqons in *Haida*, pp. 92, 95, 171. The Masset version appears in *Haida Texts*, pp. 94, 98; and the Skidegate in *Haida T. and M.*, p. 458. His name is included in some Haida family names of the Eagle phratry; see *Haida*, pp. 282–3. The name of the goddess of Fortune is Skil (*Haida Texts*, pp. 306, 665). Cf. the bird Skil, Skirl (*Haida*, p. 120). Skiltagos means copper-property and the fabulous tale of the way coppers are found is connected with this name, cf. p. 146, Fig. 4. A carved pole represents Djilqada, his copper, pole and emblems; p. 125.

The real title of Skil (ibid., p. 92) is 'property making a noise'. She has four supplementary names, ibid., p. 95. She has a son called 'Sides of Stone' (in reality copper, ibid., pp. 110, 112). Whoever meets her and her children is lucky in gambling. She has a magic plant and to eat it brings wealth; likewise one becomes rich by touching her blanket. One of her names is 'Property remaining in the House'. Many people have names which include hers: 'Attendant on Skil', 'The Way to Skil'. See Haida genealogies E 13, E 14; and in the Crow Phratry, R 14, 15, 16. She seems to be the antithesis of the 'Plague Woman' (*Haida T. and M.*, p. 299).

[183] The whole myth is given in *Tlingit T. and M.*, pp. 173, 292, 368; cf. *Tlingit*, p. 460. At Sitka Skil is doubtless Lenaxxidek. This is a woman who has a child; the child is heard suckling, and is followed. If it scratches then pieces from the scars formed can make others happy.

[184] The Tsimshian myth is incomplete: *Tsim. Myth.*, pp. 154, 192. Cf. Boas's notes, ibid., pp. 746, 760. Although Boas did not notice the identity it is clear. The Tsimshian goddess wears a 'garment of wealth'.

[185] Maybe the myth of Qominoqa, the 'rich woman', has the same origin. She seems to be the object of a cult reserved for certain Kwakiutl clans; e.g. *Eth. Kwa.*, p. 862. A Qoexsotenoq hero has the title 'Body of Stone' and becomes 'Property on the Body'; *Kwa. T.* I, p. 187.

[186] E.g. myth of the Orc Clan: Boas, *Handbook of American Languages*, Vol. I, pp. 554–9. The founder-hero of the clan is himself a member of the Orc Clan: 'I am trying to get a magical treasure from you' he says to a spirit whom he meets, which has a human shape but yet is an orc—p. 557. The spirit recognizes him as a clansman and gives him the copper-tipped whale-killing harpoon (omitted from text; orcs are killer whales). It gives him also its potlatch-name. His name, it says, is 'Place of getting Satiated, and your house with a killer whale (painting) on the front will be your house; and your dish will be a killer-whale dish; and the death-bringer and the water of life and the quartz-edged knife, which is to be your butcher-knife (shall be yours).'

[187] A wonderful box containing a whale, which gave its name to a hero, was called 'Wealth from the Shore', *Sec. Soc.*, p. 374. Cf. 'Property drifting towards me', ibid., pp. 247, 414. Property 'makes a noise' (see above). The title of one of the principal Masset chiefs is 'He whose Property makes a noise', *Haida Texts*, p. 684. Property lives (Lwakinol): 'May our property remain alive by his efforts, may our copper remain unbroken', sing the Maamtagila, *Eth. Kwa.*, p. 1285.

[188] Family possessions that circulate among men and their daughters and sons-in-law and return to the sons when newly initiated or married

are usually kept in a box or trunk adorned with emblems, whose design, construction and use are characteristic of these civilizations—from the Californian Yurok to the tribes of the Behring Straits. Usually the box is decorated with figures or eyes of the totems or spirits whose effects it contains—decorated blankets, 'death' and 'life' charms, masks, hats, crowns and bow. Myths often confuse the spirit with the box and its contents; e.g. *Tlingit T. and M.*, p. 173: the *gonaqadet* is identified with the box, the copper, hat and bell rattle. Its transfer at initiation makes the recipient a 'supernatural' being—shaman, magician, nobleman, owner of dances or seats in a fraternity. See family histories in *Eth. Kwa.*, pp. 965–6, cf. p. 1012.

The box is always mysterious and kept secretly in the house. There may be a number of boxes each in turn containing a smaller one. For Haida see *Haida Texts*, p. 395. It contains such spirits as the 'Mouse Woman' (*Haida T. and M.*, p. 340), or the Crow that pecks the eyes of an unlawful possessor. See *Tsim. Myth.*, pp. 851, 854. The myth of the sun enclosed in a floating box is widespread (ibid., pp. 549, 641). These myths are known also from the ancient world.

A common episode of legends of heroes is that of the small box containing a whale which only the hero is able to lift: *Sec. Soc.*, p. 374 and *Kwa. T.* II, p. 171; its food is inexhaustible—ibid., p. 223. The box is alive, and floats in the air through its own vitality—*Sec. Soc.*, p. 374. The box of Katlian brings wealth—*Tlingit*, pp. 446, 448. The talismans it contains have to be fed. One of them contains a spirit 'too strong to be appropriated', whose mask kills the bearer (*Tlingit T. and M.*, p. 341).

The names of these boxes refer sometimes to their use at a potlatch. A large Haida box of fat is the 'mother' (*Haida Texts*, p. 758). The red-bottomed box (the sun) distributes water on to the 'sea of tribes'—the water being the blankets which a chief distributes; *Sec. Soc.*, p. 551.

The mythology of the magic box is characteristic also of Asiatic societies of the North Pacific. There is a good comparable example in Pilsudski, *Material for the Study of the Ainu Languages*, Cracow, 1913, pp. 124–5. The box is given by a bear and the hero has taboos to observe; it is full of gold and silver objects, wealth-giving talismans. The design of the box is the same here also.

[189] Family possessions are individually named among the Haida—Swanton, *Haida*, p. 117;—houses, doors, dishes, carved spoons, canoes, salmon traps. Cf. the expression 'continuous chain of possessions'—ibid., p. 15. We have a list of objects named by the Kwakiutl by clans in addition to the variable titles of nobles, men and women, and their privileges—dances, etc., which are also possessions. The things we call movables and which are personified are dishes, the house, dog and canoe; *Eth. Kwa.*, pp. 793 ff. Hunt forgot coppers, abalone shells and doors from the list. Spoons threaded to a cord on a kind of decorated canoe are called 'anchor-lines' of spoons. *Sec. Soc.*, p. 422. Among the Tsimshian, canoes, coppers, spoons, stone pots, stone knives and plates of chieftainesses are named: *Tsim. Myth.*, p. 506.

[190] The only domestic animal in these tribes is the dog. It is named

according to the clan and cannot be sold. 'They are men like us' say the Kwakiutl (*Eth. Kwa.*, p. 1260). They 'guard the family' against sorcery and attacks of enemies. A myth tells how a Koskimo chief and his dog Waned change places and use the same name, ibid., p. 835. Cf. the fantastic myth of the four dogs of Lewiqilaqu, *Kwa. T.* I, pp. 18, 20.

[191] 'Abalone' is the Chinook word for the large haliotis shells used as nose and ear ornaments (*Kwakiutl*, p. 484; and *Haida*, p. 146). They are also used on decorated blankets, belts and hats, e.g. *Eth. Kwa.*, p. 1069. Among the Awekinoq and Lasiqoala (Kwakiutl group) abalone shells are set into a shield of strangely European design; *5th Report*, p. 43. This kind of shield is akin to the copper shield which also has a suggestion of the Middle Ages.

Abalone shells were probably used as a kind of currency in the way that coppers are used now. A Ctatlolq myth (South Salish) associates the two persons K'okois, Copper and Teadjas, Abalone; their son and daughter marry and the grandson takes the 'metal box' of the bear, and appropriates his mask and potlatch: *Indianische Sagen*, p. 84. An Awikenoq myth connects shell names, like copper names, with the 'Daughters of the Moon', ibid., pp. 218-9.

Among the Haida these shells—the famous and valuable ones at least —have their own names as in Melanesia: Swanton, *Haida*, p. 146. They are also used for naming people or spirits, e.g. index of proper names in *Tsim. Myth.*, p. 960. Cf. 'abalone names' by clans in *Eth. Kwa.*, pp. 1261–75 for the tribes Awikenoq, Naqoatok and Gwasela. This custom was widespread. The abalone box of the Bella Coola is itself mentioned and described in the Awikenoq myth; moreover, it contains the abalone blanket, and both are as bright as the sun. The chief whose myth contains the story is Legek—*Indianische Sagen*, pp. 218 ff. This is the title of the principal Tsimshian chief. It would appear that the myth has travelled along with the thing itself. In the Masset Haida myth, 'Crow the Creator', the sun which he gives his wife is an abalone shell: *Haida Texts*, pp. 227, 313. Names of mythical heroes with abalone titles in *Kwa. T.* I, pp. 50, 222, etc. With the Tlingit the shells were identified with sharks' teeth: *Tlingit T. and M.*, p. 129 (cf. use of cachalot teeth in Melanesia).

All these tribes have in addition dentalia necklaces (see Krause, *Tlinkit Indianer*, p. 186). Thus we find here the same kinds of money, with the same kinds of belief and the same customs as in Melanesia and the Pacific in general.

These shells were the object of trade by the Russians during their occupation of Alaska—trade which extended from the Gulf of California to the Behring Straits: see *Haida Texts*, p. 313.

[192] Blankets like boxes become the object of legends. Their designs are even copied on boxes (*Tlinkit Indianer*, p. 200). There is always something mystical about them: cf. Haida 'spirit belts'—torn blankets (*Haida*, pp. 165, 174). Some mythical cloaks are 'cloaks of the world' (*Indianische Sagen*, p. 248). Cf. the talking mat in *Haida Texts*, pp. 430, 432. The cult of blankets, mats and hide coverings should be compared with the Polynesian cult of decorated mats.

[193] It is admitted with the Tlingit that everything in the house speaks, that spirits talk to the posts and beams of the house, and that the latter also talk and that conversations are held between the totemic animals, the spirits, men and things of the house; this is a regular feature of Tlingit religion. See *Tlingit*, pp. 458–9. The Kwakiutl house hears and speaks— *Eth. Kwa.*, p. 1279.

[194] The house is considered as personal property as it was for a long time in Germanic law. See the many myths about the 'magic house' built in the winking of an eye, usually given by a grandfather (*Tsim. Myth.*, pp. 852–3). For Kwakiutl examples see *Sec. Soc.*, pp. 376, 380.

[195] Valuable objects, being at the same time of magical and religious value—eagle feathers, often identified with rain, food, quartz and good medicines; e.g. *Tlingit T. and M.*, p. 385; *Haida Texts*, p. 292: walking sticks and combs; *Tlingit T. and M.*, p. 385; *Haida*, p. 38; *Kwakiutl*, p. 455: bracelets, e.g. Lower Frazer tribe, *Indianische Sagen*, p. 36; *Kwakiutl*, p. 454. All these things, spoons, dishes and coppers have the generic Kwakiutl name of *logwa* which means talisman, supernatural thing (cf. our 'Origines de la Notion de la Monnaie' and the preface of our *Mélange d'Histoire des Religions*). The notion of *logwa* is precisely that of *mana*. For our purpose it is the 'virtue' of wealth and food which produces wealth and food. A discourse on the *logwa* calls it 'the great past augmenter of property' (*Eth. Kwa.*, p. 1280). A myth tells how a *logwa* was good at acquiring property, how four *logwa* gathered to it. One of them was called 'Making Property accumulate': *Kwa. T.* I, p. 108. In short, wealth begets wealth. A saying of the Haida speaks of 'property which enriches' with reference to the abalone shells worn by girls at puberty: *Haida*, p. 48.

[196] One mask is called 'Obtaining Food'. Cf.: 'and you will be rich in food' (Nimkish myth, *Kwa. T.* I, p. 36). An important Kwakiutl noble has the titles 'The Inviter', 'Giver of Food', and 'Giver of Eagle Down'; *Sec. Soc.*, p. 415.

The decorated baskets and boxes (e.g. those used for the berry crop) are likewise magical; see e.g. a Haida myth in *Haida Texts*, p. 404; the important myth of Qals confuses pike, salmon and the thunder-bird and a basket of berries seized from the bird (Lower Frazer River, *Indianische Sagen*, p. 34); equivalent Awikenoq myth, *5th Report*, p. 28; one basket is called 'Never Empty'.

[197] Each dish is named according to the carving on it. With the Kwakiutl the carvings represent 'animal chiefs'. One is 'The dish which remains full'—Boas, *Kwakiutl Tribes* (Columbia University), p. 264. Those of a certain clan are *logwa;* they have spoken to an ancestor, 'Inviter', and have told him to take them: *Eth. Kwa.*, p. 809. Cf. the myth of Kaniqilaku, *Indianische Sagen*, p. 198. Cf. *Kwa. T.* II, p. 205; how a plaguing father-in-law is given berries to eat from a magic basket. They turn into brambles and issue from all parts of his body.

[198] This German expression was used by Krickeberg. It describes the use of these shields exactly; for they are at the same time pieces of money and objects of display carried in the potlatch by chiefs or those to whose profit the potlatch is given.

[199] Although it has been widely discussed the copper industry of North-West America is not well known. Rivet in his notable work 'Orfèvrerie Précolombienne', *Journal des Américanistes*, 1923, left it out intentionally. It seems certain that the art was there before the arrival of the Europeans. The northern tribes, Tlingit and Tsimshian, sought, worked or received the native copper from the Copper River. Cf. Indian authors and Krause, *Tlinkit Indianer*, p. 186. All these tribes speak of a 'great copper mountain': *Tlingit T. and M.*, p. 160; *Haida*, p. 130; *Tsim. Myth.*, p. 299.

[200] Copper is alive: its mine and mountains are magical, covered with wealth-giving plants: *Haida Texts*, pp. 681, 692; *Haida*, p. 146. It has a smell; *Kwa. T.* I, p. 64. The privilege of working copper is the object of an important cycle of Tsimshian legends: myths of Tsanda and Gao, *Tsim. Myth.*, p. 306. For list of equivalent themes see ibid., p. 856. Copper seems to be personified with the Bella Coola—*Indianische Sagen*, p. 261. Cf. Boas, 'Mythology of the Bella Coola Indians', *J.N.P.E.*, Vol. I, pt. 2, p. 71, where the myth of copper is associated with the myth of abalone.

[201] Since it is red, copper is identified with the sun: *Tlingit T. and M.*, nos. 39, 81; with 'fire from the sky', which is the name of a copper, and with salmon. This identification is specially clear in the cult of twins among the Kwakiutl, *Eth. Kwa.*, pp. 685 ff. The sequence seems to be: springtime, arrival of salmon, new sun, red colour, copper. The identity of salmon and copper is more characteristic of the northern nations (*Tsim. Myth.*, p. 856). E.g. *Haida Texts*, pp. 689, 691, 692; here the myth is like that of the ring of Polycratus; the salmon swallows copper (*Haida T. and M.*, p. 82). The Tlingit have the myth of the being called Mouldy-End (the name of a salmon); see myth of Sitka; chains of copper and salmon (*Tlingit T. and M.*, p. 307). A salmon in a box becomes a man; another version, ibid., no. 5. See *Tsim. Myth.*, p. 857. A Tsimshian copper is 'Copper going upstream', a clear allusion to salmon.

It would be worth while investigating the relationship between the copper and quartz cults—see myth of the quartz mountain, *Kwa. T.* II, p. 111. In the same way the jade cult—at least with the Tlingit—could be related to the copper cult; a jade salmon speaks (*Tlingit T. and M.*, p. 5); a jade stone speaks and gives names, Sitka, ibid., p. 416. And note of course the association of the shell cult and copper.

[202] The family of Tsanda among the Tsimshian seems to be the founder of copper and to have its secrets. Possibly the Kwakiutl myth of the princely family of Dzawadaenoqu is of the same sort. It brings together Laqwagila the maker of copper, Qomqomgila the rich man and Qomoqoa the rich woman who makes coppers; and links them to the white bird (sun), son of the thunder-bird, who smells of copper, turns himself into a woman and gives birth to twins who smell of copper (*Kwa. T.* I, pp. 61–7).

The Awikenoq myth about ancestors and nobles who have the same title 'Maker of Copper' is less interesting.

[203] Each copper has a name. Kwakiutl speak of 'great coppers with names'—*Sec. Soc.*, pp. 348–50. We know quite a bit about the names of the great Kwakiutl coppers. They refer to the cults and beliefs attached to them. One is 'Moon' (Nisqa tribe, *Eth. Kwa.*, p. 856), others have the

name of the spirit they incarnate and which gave them, e.g. the Dzonoqoa, ibid., p. 1421. Others have names of spirits who founded totems: one copper is 'Beaver Face', ibid., p. 1427, another, 'Sea Lion', ibid., p. 894. Other names allude to the shape, e.g. 'T-shaped Copper', or 'Long Upper Portion', ibid., p. 862. Others are called simply 'Great Copper', 'Noisy Copper' (also a chief's name). The name of the Maxtoselen copper is 'That of which they are ashamed'. 'They are ashamed of their debts' (*Kwa. T.* I, p. 452; 'Quarrel Maker' (*Eth. Kwa.*, p. 893).

Most Tlingit copper names are totemic (*Tlingit*, pp. 405, 421). Of Haida and Tsimshian names, we know only of those which are the same as the names of the chiefs who own them.

²⁰⁴ The value of Tlingit coppers varies according to their size and used to be measured in slaves; *Tlingit T. and M.*, pp. 131, 260, 337. Boas studied the way in which each copper gains in value through a series of potlatches; e.g. the value of the copper Lesaxalayo about 1906–10 was 9000 woollen blankets each worth about $4, 50 canoes, 6000 blankets with buttons, 260 silver bracelets, 60 gold bracelets, 70 gold ear-rings, 40 sewing machines, 25 gramophones, 50 masks; and the herald said: 'Now he will give these poor things to you, tribes'. (*Eth. Kwa.*, p. 1352. A copper is also compared here to the 'body of a whale'.)

²⁰⁵ The destruction of coppers seems to have been carried out in a special way. Among the Kwakiutl it is done piecemeal, a part being broken with each potlatch. At later potlatches one tries to regain the broken portions for they may be riveted on to the copper again—which then grows in value; *Sec. Soc.*, p. 334. In any case to spend or break them is to 'kill' them, *Eth. Kwa.*, p. 1285. The common expression is 'to throw them into the sea': also in Tlingit (*Tlingit T. and M.*, pp. 63, 399). If the coppers do not sink or die they are wooden—they float (*Tsim. Myth.*, p. 369). Broken, they are said to have 'died on the shore' (*Sec. Soc.*, p. 564).

²⁰⁶ The Kwakiutl have two kinds of coppers: the more important which do not leave the family and which one can break only to refounder, and others which circulate intact, of less value and, as it were, satellites of the former (ibid., pp. 564, 579). The possession of these secondary coppers probably corresponds to possession of those noble titles and ranks of second order with which they travel from chief to chief, family to family, and between generations and sexes; while the big coppers and titles remain within clans and tribes.

²⁰⁷ A Haida myth on the potlatch of chief Hayas tells how a copper sings: 'But that thing is bad. . . . Stop Gamsiwa (the name of a town and a hero); there are many coppers' (*Haida Texts*, p. 760). A 'little copper' becomes 'big' of its own accord and others crowd around it. In a child's song (*Eth. Kwa.*, p. 1312) 'the coppers with great names of the great chiefs of the tribes will gather around it'. The coppers are said to 'fall by themselves into the chief's hand'. They 'meet in the house', they are the 'flat objects that collect there' (ibid., p. 701).

²⁰⁸ Cf. the myth of 'Bringer of Coppers' in the myth of 'Inviter' (Qoexsot'enox), *Kwa. T.* I, p. 248. The same copper is 'Bringer of Property', *Sec. Soc.*, p. 415. The secret song of the nobleman 'Inviter' runs: 'My name

will be "Property coming towards me" because of my "Bringer of Property". Coppers come towards me because of my "Bringer of Coppers".'

²⁰⁹ E.g. *Tlingit T. and M.*, p. 379; a Tsimshian copper is called a 'shield', *Tsim. Myth.*, p. 385. In a text on the donation of coppers in honour of a newly initiated son, the coppers are given an armour of property (*Sec. Soc.*, p. 557—allusion to coppers hung round the neck). The youth's name is Yaqois, 'Bearer of Property'.

²¹⁰ An important rite at the puberty seclusion of Kwakiutl princesses shows these beliefs. They wear coppers and abalone shells, and themselves take copper-names. It is said that they and their husbands will easily get coppers, *Eth. Kwa.*, p. 701. 'Coppers in the House' is the title of the sister of an Awikenoq hero, *Kwa. T.* I, p. 430. A Kwakiutl noble girl's song runs: 'I am seated on coppers . . . my belt has been woven by my mother, and I use it when I look after the dishes that will be given as my marriage payment. . . .' *Eth. Kwa.*, p. 1314.

²¹¹ Coppers are often identified with spirits; cf. the well-known theme of the animated shield and emblem. Identity of copper with Dzonoqoa and Qominoqa, ibid., pp. 1421, 860. Coppers are totemic animals, *Tsim. Myth.*, p. 460. In other cases they are attributes of mythical animals: 'Copper Deer' and the 'Copper Antlers' play a role in Kwakiutl summer festivals: *Sec. Soc.*, pp. 630–1; cf. p. 729: 'Greatness on his Body'. Tsimshian consider coppers as 'the hair of spirits'—ibid., p. 326—as 'excrement of spirits'— *Tsim. Myth.*, p. 387. Coppers are used in a potlatch given among spirits, ibid., p. 285. Coppers 'please them', ibid., p. 846. Cf. the song of Neqapenkem: 'I am pieces of copper, and the chiefs of the tribes are broken coppers': *Sec. Soc.*, p. 482.

²¹² The copper Dandalayu 'grunts in the house' to be given away, ibid., p. 622. The copper Maxtoslem 'complains of not being broken'. The blankets with which it is paid for keep it warm. The name means 'which other coppers are ashamed to look upon'. Another copper takes part in a potlatch and 'is ashamed', *Eth. Kwa.*, p. 882. A Haida copper, *Haida Texts*, p. 689, belonging to chief 'He whose property makes a noise' sings after being broken: 'I will decay here, I took away many people (to death through the potlatch).'

²¹³ The two rites of the giver and receiver being buried under and walking over blankets are equivalent; one is above or beneath one's wealth.

²¹⁴ General observation: We know how, why and during what ceremonies expenditure and destruction take place in North-West America, but it is not always clear exactly how the transfer of things—especially coppers—takes place. This question should be studied. The little we do know is interesting and shows the bond between property and its owner. The cession of a copper is 'to put the copper in the shadow of the name' and its acquisition 'gives weight' to the new owner (*Sec. Soc.*, p. 349). With the Haida to show that one is buying a piece of land one lifts a copper (*Haida T. and M.*, p. 86); also one beats people to whom one gives them as in the story, ibid., p. 432. Things touched by the copper are annexed to it, killed by it.

In at least one myth the Kwakiutl (*Sec. Soc.*, pp. 383–5) retain the memory of a transmission rite found also among the Eskimo; the hero bites everything he gives away. The Mouse Woman 'licks' what she gives (*Haida Texts*, p. 191).

²¹⁵ In the marriage rite of breaking the symbolic canoe, there is this song:

> 'I am going to break Mount Stevens to pieces, I shall make stones for
>   my fire
> I am going to break Mount Qatsai to pieces, I shall make stones for
>   my fire
> Wealth is on its way to him from the great chiefs
> Wealth is on its way to him from all sides
> All the big chiefs will be protected by him.'

²¹⁶ With the Kwakiutl these are normally identical. Certain nobles are identified with their potlatch. The principal chief's main title is Maxwa, meaning 'great potlatch', *Eth. Kwa.*, p. 972. In the same clan are the names 'Giver of Potlatches', etc. In another Kwakiutl tribe, the Dzawadeenoxu, one of the main titles is Polas. The principal chief of the Heiltsuq is in relations with the spirit Qominoqa, the rich woman and has the name 'Maker of Wealth', *Eth. Kwa.*, pp. 424, 427. Qaqtsenoqu princes have 'summer names'—clan names made up of the word 'property'—e.g. 'Property of the Body', 'Great Property', 'Place of Property', *Kwa. T.* I, p. 191. The Naqoatoq Kwakiutl give their chief the titles Maxwa and Yaxlem ('Property'); this name figures in the myth of 'Body of Stone'. The spirit says: 'Your name will be Property', ibid., p. 215. Also with the Haida a chief has the name 'That which cannot be bought', *Haida*, p. 294. The same chief is also 'Everything Mixed', i.e. a potlatch assembly, ibid.

Chapter III

¹ Meillet. H. Lévy-Bruhl and Huvelin contributed invaluable suggestions for the passage that follows.

² Outside the hypothetical reconstruction of the *Twelve Tables* and some laws preserved as inscriptions, our sources for the first four centuries of Roman law are very poor. We do not, however, adopt the hypercritical attitude of Lambert in 'L'Histoire traditionelle des Douzes Tables', *Mélanges Appleton*, 1906. Nevertheless, many of the theories of Romanists and Roman antiquaries should still be treated as hypotheses. It might even be permitted us to add another hypothesis to the list.

³ On the *nexum* see Huvelin, 'Nexum' in *Dictionnaire des Antiquaires;* 'Magie et Droit individuels', *A.S.*, X, and his analyses and discussions in *A.S.*, VII, 472 ff.; IX, 412 ff.; XI, 442 ff.; XII, 482 ff.; *Foi Jurée*, p. 135; bibliography and theories of Romanists, see Giraud, *Manuel élémentaire de Droit Romain*, 7th edn., p. 354.

Huvelin and Giraud appear to hold close to the truth. However, the injury clause (*Magie et Droit*, p. 28, cf. 'Injuria', *Mélanges Appleton*) is in our opinion not solely magic. It is a clear case, a trace, of former potlatch rules. The fact that the one is a debtor and the other a creditor allows the one thus in a position of superiority to injure his opponent, the man who is under an obligation to him: hence a series of joking relationships to which we drew attention in *A.S.*, New Series, I, particularly in the Winnebago tribe.

⁴ Huvelin, *Magie et Droit.*

⁵ On *wadiatio*, see Davy, *A.S.*, XII, 522–3.

⁶ Our rendering of the word *stips* is based on that of Isidore de Seville. See Huvelin, *Stips, Stipulatio* (*Mélanges Fadda*, 1906); Giraud, *Manuel*, p. 507, following Sévigny, holds the texts of Varro and Festus against such a purely metaphorical representation. Festus having spoken of *stipulus* and *firmus* mentions in a sentence in part missing, '(?) *defixus*', possibly a stick fixed in the ground; cf. throwing a stick at the sale of land in contracts of the Hammurabi period in Babylon, v. Cuq, in *Nouvelle Revue Historique de Droit*, 1910, p. 407.

⁷ See Huvelin in *A.S.*, X, 33.

⁸ We do not propose to enter the discussions of Romanists, but we would add a few observations to those of Huvelin and Giraud on the *nexum*. (1) The word is derived from *nectere* upon which Festus has preserved one of the rare documents of the Pontifices which have survived: *Napuras stramentis nectito*. The document alludes to the taboo on property indicated by knots made in straw. Thus the thing *tradita* was itself marked and tied and came to the *accipiens* with this mark on it. Thus it would bind him. (2) The person who becomes *nexus* is the receiver, *accipiens*. Now the rite of the *nexum* supposes he is *emptus*, usually translated as 'bought'. But *emptus* really means *acceptus*. The person who has received the thing is not only bought, but received also, by the loan, because he has received the thing and because he has received the copper ingot which the loan gives him as well as the thing itself. There is discussion whether there is *damnatio*, *mancipatio*, etc. in the transaction (*Manuel*, p. 503). Without entering into the argument we state our opinion that these terms are more or less synonymous. Cf. expressions *nexo mancipioque* and *emit mancipioque accepit* of the inscriptions (sale of slaves). There is no difficulty in holding this opinion since the fact of accepting a thing from someone makes you obliged to him: *damnatus, emptus, nexus.* (3) It seems that the Romanists—and Huvelin— have not paid enough attention to a formal detail of the *nexum*—what happens to the brass ingot, the *aes nexum* so much discussed in Festus. At the establishment of the *nexum* this bar is given by the donor to the recipient. But, we believe, when the latter freed himself he does so not only by making the promised prestation or by giving over the object or its price, but, more important, with the same scales and the same witnesses he returns the same bar to his creditor. Thus he buys it and receives it in its turn. This rite of the *solutio* of the *nexum* is well described in Gaius, III, 174. Since in an immediate sale the two actions happened as it were at the same time or with a very small interval, the double symbol was less noticeable than in a credit sale or in the case of a loan; hence it passed unnoticed. But it was there all the same. If our interpretation is correct there is, in addition to the *nexum* from the object of sale, another *nexum* deriving from this ingot

given and received, and weighed in the same scales by the two contractors. (4) Let us suppose, moreover, we can imagine a Roman contract before the time of bronze money or the weighed ingot or even the piece of copper in the form of a cow (*aes flatum*); we know that the first Roman money was coined by the *gentes* in the form of cattle (probably as tokens representing the cattle of these *gentes*). Let us suppose a sale where the price is paid in real or imaginary cattle. We then realize that the handing over of this cattle-price or its equivalent brought the buyer and seller together; as in each sale or transfer of cattle the person who acquires them remains for some time in contact with the person who ceded them.

⁹ Varro, *De Re Rustica*, II, 1, 15.

¹⁰ On *familia* see *Digest*, L, XVI, *de verb. sign.*, no. 195, para. 1. 'Familiae appellatio . . . et in res, et in personas diducitur . . .' (Ulpian). Until late in Roman law the action of the division of inheritance is called *familiae erciscundae*, *Digest*, XI, II, and the Code, III, XXXVIII. Inversely *res* equals *familia; Twelve Tables*, V, 3, 'super pecunia tutelave suae rei'. Cf. Giraud, *Textes de Droit romain*, p. 869; Cuq, *Institutions*, I, 37. Gaius, II, 224 reproduces this text: 'super familia pecuniaque'. *Familia* equals *res* and *substantia*—cf. Code (Justinian) VI, XXX, 5. Cf. *familia rustica et urbana*, *Digest*, L, XVI, *de verb. sign.*, no. 166.

¹¹ Cicero, *De Orat.*, 56: *pro Caecina*, VII. Terence, 'decem dierum vix mihi est familia'.

¹² *Walde*, p. 70. Although Walde hesitates over the proposed etymology, there is no need. The principal *res*, the real *mancipium* of the *familia* is the *mancipium* slave whose other name, *famulus*, has the same etymology as *familia*.

¹³ On the distinction *familia pecuniaque* attested by the *sacratae leges* and by numerous texts, see Giraud, *Textes*, p. 841. It is certain the nomenclature was not very definite, yet contrary to Giraud we believe that originally there was a clear distinction. The distinction is found in the Oscan *famelo in eituo* (*Lex Bantia*, l. 13).

¹⁴ This distinction did not disappear from Roman law until A.D. 532 when it was expressly abrogated.

¹⁵ On *mancipatio* see later. The fact that it was necessary, or at least licit, until so late a date shows how difficult it was for the *familia* to do without *res mancipi*.

¹⁶ On this etymology see *Walde*, p. 650. Cf. *rayih*, property, valuable thing, talisman. Cf. Avestic *rae*, *rayyi*, same meanings; cf. old Irish *rath*, gracious gift.

¹⁷ The Oscan word for *res* is *egmo*, cf. *Lex Bantia*. Walde connects *egmo* with *egere*, the thing one lacks. Possibly ancient Italic languages had two corresponding and antithetical words meaning a thing which one gives and which gives pleasure (*res*) and the thing lacked and which one expects (*egmo*).

¹⁸ See Huvelin, '*Furtum*' (*Mélanges Girard*), pp. 159–75.

¹⁹ Expression of a very old law, *lex Atinia*, XVII, 7: 'Quod subruptum erit ejus rei aeterna auctoritas est.' Cf. Ulpian III, 4 and 6. Cf. Huvelin, *Magie et Droit*, p. 19.

²⁰ With the Haida the victim of a theft places a dish before the thief's door and the thing returns.

²¹ Giraud, *Manuel*, p. 265. Cf. *Digest*, XIX, IV, *de Permut.*: 'permutatio autem ex re tradita initium obligationi praebat.'

²² *Mod. Regul.* in *Digest*, XLIV, VII, *de Obl. et act.*, 52, 're obligamur cum res ipsa intercedit.'

²³ Justinian, *Code* VIII, LVI.

²⁴ Paul, *Digest*, XLI, 1–31.

²⁵ *Code* II, III, *de Pactis* 20.

²⁶ On the meaning of *reus*, guilty, responsible, see Mommsen, *Römisches Strafrecht*, 3rd edn., p. 189. The classic interpretation comes from a sort of historical a-priorism which makes public personal law and in particular criminal law the primitive form of law, and which sees real law and contracts as modern refinements.

Reus belongs to the language of religion (v. Wissowa, *Religion und Kultus der Römer*, p. 320) no less than to the language of law: *voti reus* (*Aeneid*, V, 327) 'reus qui voto se numinibus obligat' (*Servius ad Aen.*, IV, 699). The equivalent of *reus* is *voti damnatus* (Virgil, *Eclogues*, V, 1, 80); and this is suggestive since *damnatus* equals *nexus*. A person who makes a vow is in the same position as one who has promised or received a thing. Until he is acquitted he is *damnatus*.

²⁷ *Indo-Germanische Forschungen*, XIV, 131.

²⁸ *Walde*, p. 651 at *reus*. This is the interpretation of Roman lawyers themselves (Cicero, *de Orat.* II, 183, 'Rei omnes quorum de re disceptatur'); they all implied by *res* an affair present to the mind. It is reminiscent of the *Twelve Tables*, II, 2, where *reus* does not mean simply the accused, but both parties in any action—the *actor* and the *reus* of later procedures. Festus commenting on the *Twelve Tables* cites two very early jurisconsults on the subject. Cf. Ulpian, *Digest*, II, XI, 2, 3, 'alterutur ex litigatoribus'.

²⁹ To the very early Roman jurisconsults cited by Festus *reus* still means a person responsible for, made responsible by, something.

³⁰ In the *Lex Bantia* in Oscan *minstreis* equals *minoris partis* (l. 19), the party which fails in the action. The meaning of these terms was not lost in Italic dialects.

³¹ Romanists seem to put the distinction between *mancipatio* and *emptio venditio* too early. It is unlikely that at the time of the *Twelve Tables*, or even for some time after that, there were contracts of sale which were pure consensual contracts as they later became at a period one can date roughly as being that of Q. M. Scaevola. The *Twelve Tables* use the phrase '*venum dunit*' to mean the most dignified sale possible and which could certainly be made only by means of *mancipatio*—the sale of a son. For things *mancipi* at this period sale was exclusively by means of *mancipatio* and our terms were thus synonymous. The Ancients retained a memory of this identity; v. Pomponius, *Digest* XL, VII, *de statu liberis*: 'Quoniam Lex XII T. emtionis verbo omnem alienationem complexa videatur'. On the other hand, for a long period the word *mancipatio* meant acts which are pure consensual contracts like *fiducia*, with which it is occasionally confused.

See Giraud, *Manuel*, p. 545. No doubt *mancipatio*, *mancipium* and *nexum* were, at a very early date, used indifferently.

Nevertheless, while noting the synonymity, we consider in what follows only *mancipatio* of those *res* which form part of the *familia* and we depart from the principle given by Ulpian, XIX, 3: 'Mancipatio . . . propria alienatio rerum mancipi.'

³² For Varro *emptio* means *mancipatio*: II, 1, 15; 2, 5; 5, 11; 10, 4.

³³ It may be that this *traditio* was accompanied by rites like those in the formality of *manumissio*, the liberation of a slave who purchases his own freedom. We are ill informed on the behaviour of the two parties to *mancipatio*. It is remarkable that the formula of *manumissio* is basically the same as that of the *emptio venditio* of cattle. Perhaps after taking up the thing to be handed over the *tradens* hit it with the palm of his hand. Cf. *vus rave*—the rap given to a pig (Banks Is., Melanesia), and the slap given in European fairs to the cruppers of cattle sold. We would not risk these hypotheses if the texts (particularly Gaius) were not full of gaps which will probably be filled later by the discovery of more manuscripts. Note also that this rite is identical with the beating of Haida coppers.

³⁴ Cuq, *Institutions Juridiques des Romains*, Vol. II, p. 454.

³⁵ The *stipulatio*, the exchange of two pieces of a stick, corresponding to former pledges and supplementary gifts.

³⁶ Festus, at *manumissio*.

³⁷ Varro, *de re rustica*, 2, i, 15; 2, v, 11: *sanis, noxis salutos*, etc.

³⁸ Note also the expressions *mutui datio*, etc. The Romans had only one word *dare* to express all the actions implied in *traditio*.

³⁹ Walde, p. 253.

⁴⁰ *Digest*, XVIII, I, 33.

⁴¹ On words of this kind see Ernout, 'Credo-Craddha' (*Mélanges Sylvain Lévi*, 1911): another case of identity between Italo-Celtic and Indo-Iranian vocabularies. Note the archaic form of all these words.

⁴² See *Walde, vendere*. Perhaps the very old term *licitatio* is a reminder that war and sale are equivalent: 'licitati in mercando sive pugnando contendentes' says Festus at *licitati*: cf. Tlingit and Kwakiutl 'war of property'.

⁴³ We have not given enough attention to Greek law or the law which preceded the great Ionic and Doric codifications, so we cannot say whether or not the various peoples of Greece knew these rules of the gift. It would be necessary to review a complete literature, but we can mention one point at present: Aristotle, *Nicomachean Ethics*, 1123, refers to the magnanimous citizen, his public and private expenses, his duties and responsibilities, and mentions reception of strangers, embassies, καὶ δωρεὰς καὶ ἀντιδωρεάς, how they expend εἰς τὰ κοινά; and he adds τὰ δὲ δῶρα τοῖς ἀναθήμασιν ἔχει τι ὅμοιον—gifts have some analogy with consecrations.

Two other living Indo-European systems of law present this kind of institution, Albanian and Ossetian. We simply make mention here of the modern laws or decrees prohibiting or limiting, among these people, excessive waste on occasions of marriage, death, etc.: Kovalewski, *Coutume contemporaine et Loi ancienne*, p. 187.

Most forms of contract are attested to on Aramaic papyri of the Jews of Philae in Egypt, fifth century B.C. See Cowley, *Aramaic Papyri*, Oxford, 1923. Note also work of Ungnad on Babylonian contracts (see Huvelin, *A.S.*, XII, p. 108 and Cuq, 'Etudes sur les Contrats . . .', *Nouvelle Revue de l'Histoire du Droit*, 1910.

⁴⁴ Ancient Hindu law is known to us through two collections published late in comparison with the rest of the scriptures. The oldest series is *Dharmasutra* which Bühler dates anterior to Buddhism ('Sacred Laws' in *Sacred Books of the East*, intro.). But it may be that some of the sutras, or the period in which they were founded, were post-Buddhic. In any case they are a part of the Hindu *Cruti*, Revelation. The other series is the *Smrti*, the Tradition, or the *Dharmacastra*: Books of the Law in which the most important is the famous Manu code which is slightly later than the sutras.

We prefer to use a long epic document which, in Brahminic tradition, has the value of *Smrti* and *Castra*. The *Anuc.* is more explicit on gift customs than the law books. Moreover, it has equal authority and the same inspiration. It seems to have the same tradition of the Brahminic school of the Manava as that upon which the Manu code itself is based (see Bühler, *The Laws of Manu*). Indeed the *parvan* and Manu code would seem to quote each other.

The book is an enormous epic on gifts. It is very popular in India. The poem relates how it was recited in tragic circumstances to Yudhisthira, the great king and incarnation of Dharma, by the seer-king Bhisma, on his bed of arrows at the time of his death.

⁴⁵ It is clear that if not the rules, at least the publication of the *castras* and epics are posterior to the struggle against Buddhism to which they refer. The *Anuc.* is full of references to Buddhism (see specially *Adhyaya*, 120). Perhaps indeed the definitive publication was as late as to allow allusion to Christianity in reference to the theory of gifts in the same *parvan*, 114, where Vyasa adds: 'That is the law subtly taught . . . that he does naught to others which he would not have done to himself—that is the law (*dharma*) in brief' (l. 5673). On the other hand, it is conceivable that the Brahmins, so fond of proverbs and dicta, arrived themselves at this idea. The preceding line has a notably Brahminic flavour: 'Such a one takes desire as his guide (and is wrong). In the refusal and in the gift, in luck and in misfortune, in pleasure and in misery it is in refusing (things) to himself that a man measures them.' The commentary of Nilakawtha is not Christian: 'As one behaves to others, so (others behave to him). It is by feeling how one would take a refusal after having solicited . . . that one sees it is necessary to give.'

⁴⁶ We do not mean that from the very ancient days of the publication of the *Rg Veda* the Aryans in North-East India had no concept of the market, merchant, price, money or sale (see Zimmern, *Altindisches Leben*, pp. 257 ff.): *Rg Veda*, IV, 24, 9. The *Atharva Veda* is familiar with this economy. Indra himself is a merchant (*Kaucika-sutra*, VII, 1, Hymn III, 15, the ritual of a man going to a sale).

Nor do we infer that this was the only origin of the contract in India, nor that India had no other forms of obligation. We seek only to show the existence, beside these laws, of another system.

⁴⁷ In particular there must have been—as with the aborigines today—total prestation of clans and villages. The prohibition on Brahmins (*Vasistha*, 14, 10 and *Gautama*, XIII, 17; *Manu*, IV, 217) against accepting anything from 'crowds', partaking in feasts offered by them, certainly points to customs of this sort.

⁴⁸ E.g. the *adanam*, gifts made by friends to parents of young initiates, betrothed persons, etc., is identical, even in name, to the Germanic *Gaben* which we mention later (see Oldenburg, *Sacred Books of India*, in *Grhyasutra* (domestic ritual). Another example, honour from gifts (of food), *Anuc.*, l. 5850: 'Honoured, they honour, decorated, they decorate, the giver everywhere is glorified.'

⁴⁹ An etymological and semantic study would provide results analogous to those we obtained on Roman law. The oldest Vedic documents are full of words whose derivations are even clearer than those of the Latin words we discussed, and all presuppose—even those concerning the market and sale—another system where exchanges, gifts and wagers took the place of the contracts we normally think of when we speak of these matters. Much has been made of the uncertainty (general in Indo-European languages) of the meaning of the Sanskrit word which we translate as 'to give'—*da*, and its numerous derivatives.

Another example we may take are the Vedic words which best represent the technical act of sale; these are *parada culkaya*, to sell at a price, and all the words derived from *pan*, e.g. *pani*, merchant. *Parada* includes *da*, and *culka*, which has the technical sense of the Latin *pretium*, means actually price of a fiancée, payment for sexual services, tax and tribute. *Pan* which gives *pani* (merchant, greedy, and a name for strangers) in the *Rg Veda*, and the word for money, *pana*, later *karsapana*, means to sell as well as gamble, bet, struggle for something, give, exchange, risk, dare, gain, stake. *Pana*, money, means also thing sold, payment, object of bet or gamble, gambling house and alms-house. This vocabulary links ideas which are found together only in the potlatch. They reveal the original system upon which was based the later system of sale and purchase in its proper sense. But this etymological reconstruction is unnecessary with Hindu material.

⁵⁰ See résumé of the epic in *Mahabharata, Andiparvan*, 6.

⁵¹ See, e.g., the legend of Hariccandra, *Subha-parvan, Mahabharata*, Book II, 12; and *Virata-parvan*, 72.

⁵² We must admit that on the obligation to make return gifts—our main subject—there are few facts from Hindu law except perhaps in *Manu*, VIII, 213. The clearest reference consists in a rule forbidding the return of gifts. It seems that originally the funerary *craddha*, the feast of the dead so highly developed by the Brahmins, was an opportunity to invite oneself and to make invitations in return. It was formally forbidden to proceed in this manner. *Anuc.*, 4311, 4315: 'He who invites only friends to the *craddha* does not go to heaven. One must invite neither friends nor enemies, but neutrals.' This prohibition was probably revolutionary. But the poet connects it with a definite school and period (*Vaikhansa Cruti*, l. 4323).

Evil Brahmins in fact oblige the gods and spirits to make returns on presents given them. Most people doubtless continued to invite friends to the festival—and they still do so in India. But although the Brahmins did not return presents, did not invite—indeed did not receive—there are plenty of documents in their codes to illustrate our case.

⁵³ *Vasistha Dharma*, XXIX, 1, 8, 9, 11–19. Cf. *Anuc.*, 64–9. This whole section seems to be a sort of litany; it is part astrological and starts with a *danakalpa* determining the constellations beneath which what people should give what things.

⁵⁴ *Anuc.*, 3212: even food offered to dogs, or to one who cooks for dogs, *cvapaka*. See the general principles on the way in which one regains things given away in the series of reincarnations; sanction on the miser, who is reborn in a poor family (XIII, 145).

⁵⁵ *Anuc.*, 3135, cf. 3162.

⁵⁶ This whole *parvan*, this song of Mahabharata is an answer to the question: how does one acquire Fortune, Cri, the unstable goddess? A first answer is that Cri lives among cattle, in their dung and their urine, where the cattle, as goddesses, have permitted her to reside. Thus to give a cow assures happiness (l. 82). A second answer, fundamentally Hindu (l. 163), teaches that the secret of Fortune and Happiness is to give, not to keep, not to seek but to distribute it that it may return in this world of its own accord in the form of the gift rendered and in the other world. Self-renunciation and getting only to give, this is the law of nature, the real source of profit (5657): 'Every man should make his days fertile by giving away food.'

⁵⁷ 3136—this stanza is called a *gatha*. It is not a *cloka;* thus it derives from an ancient tradition. I believe, moreover, that the first half-line *mamevadattha, mam dattha, mam dattva mamevapsyaya* can be taken separately from the second. Line 3132 does so in advance: 'Like a cow running to her calf, her udders dropping milk, so the blessed earth runs towards the earth-giver.'

⁵⁸ *Baudhayana Dh.*, su. 11, 18—contemporary not only with these rules of hospitality but also with the cult of food, which can be said to be contemporary with later forms of Vedic religion and to have lasted until Vishnuism when it disintegrated. *Angihotra* are Brahminic sacrifices, late Vedic period. Cf. *Baudh. Dh.*, su. 11, 6, 41–2; cf. *Taittiriya Aranyaka*, VIII, 2.

⁵⁹ The whole thing is exposed in the intercourse between the *rsi* Maitreya and Vyasa, the incarnation of Krsna Draipayana (*Anuc.*, XIII, 120–1). Here there is a trace of the struggle between Brahminism and Buddhism (l. 5802); and also allusion to a period where Krishnaism is victorious. But the doctrine is ancient Brahminic theology and the most ancient morality of India.

⁶⁰ Ibid., 5831. Read the Calcutta edition *annam* in place of the Bombay *artham*. The second half-line is obscure: 'This food which he eats, in whom it is food, he is the assassin who is killed, the fool.' The two following lines are also enigmatic but express the idea more clearly and allude to a doctrine that had a name, that of a *rsi* (5834): 'The wise man eating food gives it rebirth, and in its turn, food gives him rebirth' (5863). 'For the merit of

the donor is the merit of the recipient (and vice versa) for here is but one wheel turning in one direction.' The rendering of *Pratap* (*Mahabharata*) is much paraphrased but based on good commentaries.

[61] *Atharvaveda*, V, 18, 3.

[62] I, 5, 16; cf. above *aeterna auctoritas* of the stolen *res*.

[63] 70. Reference is to a gift of cattle, of which the ritual is given in 69.

[64] 'The property of the Brahmin kills like the cow of the Brahmin (kills) Nrga'—l. 3462, cf. 3519 .

[65] *Anuc.*, 72, 76–7. These rules are given with a plethora of detail—improbable and no doubt purely theoretical. The ritual is attributed to the school of Brhaspati. It lasts three days and nights before the event and three days after it; at times it even lasts ten days (3532, 3517, 3597).

[66] He lived in a continual giving of cattle—*gavam pradana*, 3695.

[67] This is also a purifying ritual. He is delivered of all sin (3673).

[68] *Samanga* (having all his limbs), *Bahula* (broad, fat), l. 3670. Cf. l. 6042, the cattle say: '*Bahula, Samanga*. You have no fear, you are pacified, you are a good friend.' The epic mentions that these are names from the *Veda* and *Cruti*. The sacred names are in fact found in *Atharvaveda*, V, 4, 18.

[69] 'Giver of you, I am giver of myself', 3676.

[70] The act of taking; the word is like *accipere*, λαμβάνειν, etc.

[71] Line 3677. The ritual shows that one can offer cattle 'in the shape of a cake of simsim or rancid butter' or in gold or silver; in which case these were treated as real cattle (3523, 3839). The rites of the transaction are rather better perfected. Ritual names are given to these cattle; one means 'the Future'. The sojourn among cattle and the 'cattle oath' are marked.

[72] *Ap. Dh.*, su. I, 17; *Manu*, X, 86–95. The Brahmin can sell what has not been bought.

[73] *Ap. Dh.*, su. I, 18, 1; *Gautama Dh.*, su. XVII, 3. Cf. *Anuc.*, 93–4.

[74] *Ap. Dh.*, su. I, 19, where Kanva, another Brahminic school, is quoted.

[75] *Manu*, IV, p. 233.

[76] *Gautama Dh.*, su. XVII, 6, 7; *Manu*, IV, 253. List of people from whom the Brahmins may not receive: *Gautama Dh.*, XVII, cf. *Manu*, IV, 215–7.

[77] List of things that must be refused: *Ap.*, I, 18; *Gautama*, XVII. Cf. *Manu*, IV, 247–50.

[78] *Anuc.*, 136; cf. *Manu*, IV, p. 250; X, pp. 101–2; *Ap. Dh.*, I, 18, 5–8; *Gautama*, VII, 4–5.

[79] *Baudh. Dh.*, su. 11, 5, 8; Recitation of Taratsamandi, as *Rg Veda*, IX, 58.

[80] 'The energy and brilliance of the sages are spoiled by the fact that they receive'. 'Guard thyself, O King, from those who will not receive' (*Anuc.*, 2164).

[81] *Gautama*, XVII, 19; *Ap.*, I, 17. Etiquette of the gift, *Manu*, VII, p. 86.

[82] *Krodho hanti yad danam*, 'Anger kills the gift', *Anuc.*, 3638.

[83] *Ap.*, II, 6, 19; cf. *Manu*, III, 5, 8, with absurd theological interpretation: 'one eats the fault of one's host'. This refers to the general prohibition on Brahmins against exercising an essential trade which they still

exercise, although they are reputed not to—the 'eating' of sins. This would mean that no good came of the gift for either of the parties.

⁸⁴ One is reborn in the other world with the nature of those whose food one accepts, or of those whose food is in one's stomach, or with the nature of the food itself.

⁸⁵ The whole theory is summed up in the fairly late *Anuc.*, 131, under the title of *danadharma* (6278): 'What gifts, to whom, when and by whom'. The five motives of gift-giving are set out: duty, when one gives spontaneously to Brahmins; self-interest ('he gives me, he gave me, he will give me'); fear ('I am not his, he is not mine, he could harm me'); love ('he is dear to me and I to him'—'he gives without delay'); and pity ('he is poor and is satisfied with little').

⁸⁶ Line 5834. One might also study the ritual by which the thing given is purified—which is also clearly a means of detaching it from the donor. It is sprinkled with water by means of a blade of grass, *kuca*. For food see *Gautama*, V, 21, 18–9; *Ap.*, II, 9, 8. Cf. water purifying debt, *Anuc.*, 69, 21, and comments, *Pratap*, p. 313.

⁸⁷ The data are fairly recent: our *Edda* songs date from a time after the conversion of the Scandinavians to Christianity. But the age of the tradition may be much earlier, and even the oldest known form of the tradition may differ from the institutions themselves. But there is no danger in the use of the facts; for some of the gifts which have such an important place in the customs we describe are among the earliest institutions observed among the Germanic tribes. Tacitus describes two forms: marriage gifts and the way in which they return to the givers (*Germania*, XVIII); and gifts of noblemen, particularly those given to or by chiefs (ibid., XV). If these customs remained as long as to enable us to observe traces of them it means surely that they were solidly implanted in Germanic society.

⁸⁸ See Schräder and his references in *Reallexikon der Indogermanisches Altertumskunde* under *Markt, Kauf*.

⁸⁹ *Kauf* and its derivatives come from the Latin *caupo*, merchant. The doubt about the meanings of the words *leihen, lehnen, Lohn, bürgen, borgen*, etc., is recognized and shows that their technical use is recent.

⁹⁰ Here we do not raise the question of *geschlossene Hauswirtschaft*—closed economy—cf. Bücher, *Entstehung der Volkswirtschaft*. There were two clans in a society and they must have made contracts and exchanges not only of wives (exogamy) and ritual, but also of goods at certain periods of the year and on certain occasions. The rest of the time the family lived to itself, but it never lived to itself at all seasons.

⁹¹ See Kluge and other etymological dictionaries of the Germanic languages. See Von Amira on *Abgabe, Ausgabe, Morgengabe* (*Handbuch Hermann Paul*).

⁹² The best works are still: J. Grimm, '*Schenken und Geben*', *Kleine Schriften*, Vol. II, p. 174; Brunner, *Deutsche Rechtsbegriffe besch. Eigentum*. See also Grimm, *Deutsche Rechtsalterthümer*, Vol. I, p. 246, cf. p. 297 on *Bete, Gabe*. The hypothesis on the development of the obligatory from the unconditional gift is untenable. Both kinds have always existed and in German law their character has always been fused.

[93] 'Zur Geschichte des Schenkens', Steinhausen *Zeitschrift für Kultur-geschichte*, V, 18 ff.

[94] E. Mayer, *Deutsche Volkskunde*, pp. 115, 168, 181, 183, and all hand-books of Germanic folklore.

[95] Here is another answer to van Ossenbruggen's query on the magical and legal nature of bridewealth. See the theory on the many prestations made to or by spouses in Morocco in Westermarck, *Marriage Ceremonies in Morocco*, pp. 361 ff.

[96] In what follows we keep the pledge distinct from the *arrhes* although this, of Semitic origin (as the Greek and Latin words indicate) was known to later Germanic law. It has even become confused with 'gift', e.g. *Handgeld* is *Harren* in some Tyrolese dialects.

We omit to show also the importance of the notion of the pledge in marriage: we simply remark that in some Germanic dialects bridewealth is *Pfand, Wetten, Trugge* and *Ehehalter*.

[97] *A.S.*, IX, 29 ff. Cf Kovalewski, *Coutume contemporaine et Loi ancienne*, pp. 111 ff.

On the Germanic *wadium*, see Thévenin, 'Contributions a l'étude du Droit germanique', *Nouv. Rev. Hist. Droit*, IV, 72; Grimm, *Deutsche Rechts-alterthümer*, Vol. I, pp. 209–13; Von Amira, 'Obligationen Recht', *Hdb. Hermann Paul*, Vol. I, pp. 248, 254. On *wadiatio*, see Davy, *A.S.*, XII, pp. 522 ff.

[98] Brissaud, *Manuel d'Histoire du Droit français*, 1904, p. 1381. Huvelin interprets this fact as a degeneration of the primitive magical rite into a simple moral theme; but this is only a partial explanation and does not exclude the possibility of our proposals.

[99] We return later to the derivations of 'wedding' and '*Wette*'. The ambiguity of 'wager' and 'contract' is notable even in French, e.g. *se défier* and *défier*.

[100] On *festuca notata* see Heusler, *Institutionen*, Vol. I, pp. 76 ff. Huvelin neglects the custom of tallies.

[101] *Mélanges Ch. Andler*, Strasburg, 1924. We are asked why we do not examine the etymology of gift as coming from the Latin *dosis*, Greek δόσις, a dose (of poison). It would suppose that High and Low German had retained a scientific word for a common event, and this is contrary to normal semantic rules. Moreover, one would have to explain the choice of the word *Gift*. Finally, the Latin and Greek *dosis*, meaning poison, shows that with the Ancients as well there was association of ideas and moral rules of the kind we are describing.

We compare the uncertainty of the meaning of *Gift* with that of the Latin *venenum* and the Greek φίλτρον and φάρμακον. Cf. also *venia, venus, venenum—vanati* (Sanskrit, to give pleasure) and *gewinnen* and win.

[102] *Reginsmal*, 7. The gods have killed Otr, son of Hreidmar, and have been obliged to redeem themselves by covering Otr's skin with gold. But the god Loki curses the gold, and Hreidmar answers with the words quoted. We owe this observation to Cohen who notes that 'of a benevolent heart' —*af heilom hug*—actually means 'of a lucky disposition'.

[103] The Chinese law of real estate, like Germanic and old French law, recognizes the right which relatives—even distant—have to repurchase property which ought not to have passed from the hereditary line; see Hoang, 'Notions techniques sur la Propriété en Chine', *Variétés sinologues*, 1897, pp. 8, 9. We do not pay much attention to this. The sale of land is a recent thing, specially in China. Up to the time of Roman law, and again in old French and Germanic laws, it was surrounded by restrictions deriving from community in family life, and the profound attachment of family to land and vice versa. Old and new laws concerning the homestead, and recent French legislation on inalienable family property, are a perpetuation of an ancient state of affairs.

[104] Hoang, ibid., pp. 10, 109, 133. I owe these facts to Mestre and Granet.

[105] *Origin and Development of Moral Ideas*, Vol. I, p. 594. Westermarck felt that there was a problem of the sort we are tackling but treated it only from the point of view of laws of hospitality. Read, however, his important observation on the Moroccan custom of *ar* (sacrifice occasioning constraint to the supplicant, p. 386) and on the principle: 'God and food will pay him' (remarkably similar to Hindu). *Marriage Ceremonies in Morocco*, p. 365; cf. *Anthropological Essays to E. B. Tylor*, pp. 373 ff.

Chapter IV

[1] Cf. *Koran*, sura II; cf. Kohler in *Jewish Encyclopedia*, Vol. I, p. 465.

[2] William James, *Principles of Psychology*, Vol. II, p. 409.

[3] Kruyt, *Koopen*, p. 12 of extract, for similar facts from Celebes. Cf. '*De Toradja's . . .*', *Tijd. v. Kon. Batav. Gen.*, LXIII, 2, p. 299: rite for bringing buffalo to stable; p. 296, ritual for buying a dog limb by limb; p. 281, the cat is not sold, on any pretext, but loans itself.

[4] Of course we do not imply any destruction; the legal principles of the market, of buying and selling, which are the indispensable conditions for the formation of capital, can and must exist beside other new and old principles.

Yet the moralist and legislator should not be bound in by so-called principles of natural law. The distinction between real and personal law should be considered as a theoretical abstraction derived from *some* of our laws. It should be allowed to exist, but kept in its proper place.

[5] Roth, 'Games' in *Bulletin of the Ethnology of Queensland*, no. 28, p. 23. The announcement of the name of the visiting clan is a common custom in East Australia and is connected with the honour and virtue of the name. The last sentence suggests that betrothals are contracted through the exchange of gifts.

[6] Radin, 'Winnebago Tribe', *A.R.B.A.E.*, XXXVII, 320 ff. See article 'Etiquette' in Hodge, *Handbook of American Indians*.

[7] Ibid., p. 326. Exceptionally two chiefs invited were members of the Snake Clan. Cf. almost identical speeches in a funeral feast: *Tlingit T. and M.*, p. 372.

⁸ Taylor, *Te ika a Mani*, p. 130, gives this translation, but the literal rendering is probably as follows: 'As much as Maru gives, so much Maru receives, and all is well' (Maru is god of war and justice).

⁹ Bücher, *Entstehung der Volkswirtschaft*, 3rd edn., p. 73, saw these economic phenomena but underestimated their importance, reducing them all to a matter of hospitality.

¹⁰ *Argonauts*, pp. 167 ff.; *Primitive Ec.*, 1921. See Frazer's preface to *Argonauts*.

¹¹ One of the most extravagant we can quote is the sacrifice of dogs among the Chukchee. The owners of the best kennels destroy their whole teams and sledges and have to buy new ones.

¹² *Argonauts*, p. 95. Cf. Preface.

¹³ *Formes Elémentaires de la Vie religieuse*, p. 598.

¹⁴ *Digest*, XVIII, I, *de contr. emt.* Paulus explains the great Roman debate on whether or not *permutatio* was a sale. The whole passage is of interest—even the mistake which the legal scholar makes in his interpretation of Homer, *Iliad*, VII, 472–5: ὀινίοντο certainly means to buy, but Greek money was bronze, iron, skins, cows and slaves, all having predetermined values.

¹⁵ *Pol.*, Book I, 1257; note the word μεταδόσις.

¹⁶ *Argonauts*, p. 177. Note that in this case there is no sale for there is no exchange of *vaygu'a*. The Trobrianders do not go so far as to use money in exchange.

¹⁷ Ibid., p. 179; cf. p. 183 for payment of a kind of licit prostitution of unmarried girls.

¹⁸ Cf. ibid., p. 81. *Sagali* (cf. *hakari*) means distribution.

¹⁹ Cf. ibid., p. 82, in particular the gift of *urigubu* to the brother-in-law; harvest products in exchange for labour.

²⁰ The division of labour and how it works in the inter-clan Tsimshian feast is admirably described in a potlatch myth in *Tsim. Myth.*, p. 274, cf. p. 378. There are many examples like this. These economic institutions exist even with societies much less developed, e.g. Australia—the remarkable situation of a local group possessing a deposit of red ochre (Aiston and Horne, *Savage Life in C. Australia*, London, 1924, pp. 81, 130).

²¹ The equivalence in Germanic languages of the words token and *Zeichen* for money in general is a survival of these institutions. The mark on money and the pledge it is are the same thing, just as a man's signature is also a mark of his responsibility.

²² *Foi Jurée*, pp. 344 ff. In '*Des Clans aux Empires*', *Eléments de Sociologie*, Vol. I, he exaggerates the importance of these points. The potlatch is useful for establishing the hierarchy and does often establish it, but this is not a necessary element. African societies either do not have the potlatch, or have it only slightly developed, or perhaps have lost it; yet they have all possible kinds of political organization.

²³ *Argonauts*, pp. 199–201, 203. The 'mountain' here is the d'Entrecasteaux group. The canoe will sink beneath the weight of stuff brought back from the *kula;* cf. pp. 200, 441–2: play on the word 'foam'.

²⁴ We should perhaps also have studied Micronesia. There is a money and contract system of first importance especially at Yap and the Palaos. In Indo-China among the Mon-Khmer, in Assam and among the Tibeto-Burmans are also institutions of this kind. The Berbers, finally, have developed the remarkable *thaoussa* customs (Westermarck, *Marriage Ceremonies in Morocco*, see index under 'present'). Old Semitic law and Bedouin custom should also give useful material.

²⁵ See the 'ritual of beauty' in the Trobriand *kula*, *Argonauts*, pp. 334, 336: 'Our partner looks at us, sees our faces are beautiful; he throws the *vaygu'a* at us.' Cf. Thurnwald on the use of silver as ornament: *Forschungen*, Vol. III, p. 39; p. 35, the expression *Prachtbaum* to denote a man or woman decorated with money. The chief is the 'tree', I, p. 298; and the ornamented man lets forth a perfume, p. 192.

²⁶ Ibid., III, p. 36.

²⁷ *Argonauts*, p. 246.

²⁸ *Samoa-Inseln*, III, Tab. 35.

²⁹ *Layamon's Brut*, ll. 22336 ff., 9994 ff.